MAIMONIDES

MAIMONIDES

Maimonides

Faith in Reason

ALBERTO MANGUEL

Yale
UNIVERSITY
PRESS

New Haven and London

Yale University Press books may be purchased in quantity for educational,
business, or promotional use. For information, please e-mail sales.press@yale.edu
(U.S. office) or sales@yaleup.co.uk (U.K. office).

Set in Janson Oldstyle type by Integrated Publishing Solutions.
Printed in the United States of America.

Library of Congress Control Number: 2022937726
ISBN 978-0-300-21789-6 (hardcover : alk. paper)

A catalogue record for this book is available from the British Library.

This paper meets the requirements of ANSI/NISO Z39.48–1992
(Permanence of Paper).

10 9 8 7 6 5 4 3 2 1

Frontispiece: Brenda Putnam, Marble bas-relief of Maimonides, 1950.
This is one of twenty-three reliefs of great historical lawgivers in the
chamber of the U.S. House of Representatives in the United States Capitol.
(Photo: Architect of the Capitol/Wikimedia Commons)

To my father, Pablo Manguel

. . . a cry issued from his father's lips:
"Have you come at last?
And has the fealty your father expected
overcome the harsh road?"
                    —*Aeneid* 6.708–709

CONTENTS

Remember the days of old, consider the years of
many generations: ask thy father, and he will shew
thee; thy elders, and they will tell thee.

—Deuteronomy 32:7

EARLY IN 2015, my editor at Yale University Press suggested that I write one of the volumes for the Jewish Lives
series she was directing, on Moses Maimonides. I had a vague
notion of who Maimonides was (a great philosopher, a great
legislator, a great medical doctor), and I remembered the in-
triguing title of his *Guide of the Perplexed*, but little more. I
thought that Maimonides might be suitable to my condition of
permanent perplexity.

That same year I had left my house in France, packed up
my library, and sent the boxes of books to be stored at the ware-
house of my Quebec publisher in Montreal. I accepted a couple
of teaching positions in New York (a city in which I had never
lived) and settled in the small apartment of a professor on sabbatical. I began to plan my reading of Maimonides. I filled in a
reader's card at the Center for Jewish History in Manhattan, I

sifted through the shelves of Judaica at the Strand Bookstore, I got permission to take out books at the Columbia University Library. I started to read several biographies of Maimonides, histories of al-Andalus, North Africa, and Egypt, books on Arab philosophy, books on the Talmud and Jewish law, histories of medieval medicine. The more I read, the vaster my subject became.

I come from a Jewish family, but I had no idea I was Jewish until I was eight, after an anti-Semitic incident for which the bewildering accusation from a bullying classmate—"Your father likes money, doesn't he?"—had to be explained to me. A very old great-uncle, the brother of my father's mother, gave me some lessons to prepare me for my bar mitzvah, and I learned by heart a few words which I mumbled in the synagogue on my thirteenth birthday. I still remember the words "Baruch atah Adonai, Elohenu melech ha'olam," which, I discovered many decades later, were the first words of the Shehecheyanu, the Jewish prayer of thanks. If I still knew the prayer by heart, I would gratefully recite it several times a day.

Maimonides was educated in a society in which several cultures were in constant though sometimes acrimonious dialogue. The Islamic, Jewish, and to a lesser extent Christian communities interacted with and learned from one another. And even when religious politics forced Maimonides into exile from al-Andalus (his beloved Sepharad) to North Africa, from there to Christian Palestine, and finally to Egypt, he never stopped learning from the cultures he encountered in the fields of religion, philosophy, and medical science. He was a very practical man: he took up medicine as a profession once the family business failed (like Socrates, he thought it was unethical for a teacher to charge for his teaching), and in his *Epistle on Conversion* (also called *Epistle on Martyrdom* or *Letter on Apostasy*), or *Iggeret ha-Shemad*, he excused those who converted to save their lives, saying that God required us to live, not die, for our faith.

Every Jew, from the days of Exodus on, is to some degree a wanderer, and though the story of the Eternal Wanderer is, for writers as different as Homer, Dante, Camões, and Joyce, emblematic of all human life, for a Jew the legend is contaminated by the experience of persecution and suffering born of an ancestral and irrational hatred toward the inventors of monotheism. But not all wandering is due to persecution. In my case, it certainly was not, and the many places in which I have lived have never seemed to me enforced habitations. Rather, they have been, for a variety of reasons, the result of conscious choices. However, after reading about Maimonides' peregrinations, I identified with the experience of constantly changing landscapes, voices, customs, languages, and skies. I often wondered how these metamorphoses were affecting me—to what extent a change of vocabulary, of conventions of tone and style transformed my way of thinking and interpreting. I discovered that for Maimonides these changes enriched his own thoughts through contact with, for instance, the science of astronomy in Seville (possibly), Islamic legal systems in Morocco, Christian politics in Palestine, Arab medicine in Egypt. But his bedside books remained the same: the Torah, with its 613 commandments of Jewish Law, and the two Talmuds, the Jerusalem and the Babylonian. What kept changing was his dialogue with those texts through his newly acquired knowledge, enriching both his reading and his commentaries on his reading. After following Maimonides, I became more conscious of how the different experiences of place had changed me and my relationship to my books.

Someone who has not experienced transience, whether as a voluntary traveler or an enforced exile, someone rooted in one place from cradle to grave, eating nothing that has not grown within the narrow circle around his or her birthplace (as the Romans enjoined), someone who cares for nothing that is not endemic (as nationalists and Dickens's Mr. Podsnap do) must possess a wonderful single-mindedness of spirit and a stringency of purpose that would hardly allow for digressive inquiry and healthy curiosity. After reading Maimonides, I saw reflected in his writings my own mania for putting things in physical order (as in his *Mishneh Torah*), my own inability to keep my thoughts confined to the straight and narrow (as in his *Guide*), my own tendency to respond actively to things that distress me in the outside world (as in his *Epistle on Conversion*). Of course, I'm not suggesting a comparison between Maimonides' work and mine. I simply want to note that after finishing my biography of Maimonides, I became more aware of my own peculiarities and avatars, and the manner in which they might have been influenced by a wandering life.

Reading Maimonides, and following him through the various stages of his exile, I wondered particularly how he managed to survive. I know that time in exile has a peculiar quality. While it was still possible for me to travel, before the pandemic constrained us to stay indoors, I know that I measured the passing of days by the ticking of airport clocks, computer-screen hours, the spinning needles of my watch backward or forward to the correct time in the new place. But after the pandemic started, steered far from hustling crowds and honking traffic, only the sound of my own pulse marked the drift of time, like the sand in the hourglass that has sat on my desk for decades and only now has acquired for me an active role. In my childhood, time was made present by the chimes of the ormolu clock in the family living room or the shrill electric bell at school. Later, the peal of the church bells in my French village marked the passing of every hour, sounding twice (the mayor had decided) in case we hadn't begun to count them at the first chime. Much the same, the muezzin's call to prayers must have marked the hours for Maimonides throughout the days of his journeys in Morocco and Egypt. He must have reflected on the relationships governing time, space, and memory, and how each infects the other with its odd qualities: time as the destroyer, space as the container of destruction, memory as the rebuilder. Maimonides believed, following Aristotle, that time, like space and movement, is composed of atoms that because of their infinitely brief span cannot be divided (quantum physics now supports this belief). Time, space, memory, and movement were in some sense, for Maimonides, of the same nature.

I, too, confuse these concepts. In the time-broken years 2020–2021, I had the steadfast impression of living inside a time-space continuum like that described in handbooks of astrophysics, a dimension in which yesterday and tomorrow, back over there and beyond the horizon were mingled notions, like a glass full of water and ink. What I did and what I remembered doing were not the same thing. There is a sense of this, I think, in the letters Maimonides wrote from Egypt recalling the tragedy of his brother's death while trying to keep up with his duties as court physician, as well as attending to the concerns of the Jewish community. He gives the impression of everything around him being in a swirl, and he himself being caught in that swirl while struggling to be reasonable and thoughtful, beating against the stubborn current of turbulent time. He must have died of exhaustion.

Maimonides taught me also to think about repenting, and to consider *repent* an active verb with myself as both subject and object. Repentance (*teshuvah* in Hebrew) is a term difficult to translate into English. As the root of the word indicates, repentance is a return, a going back to something we have done in order to consider that action again, critically and sincerely. Repentance in this sense is the reversal of a temporal glitch, making it possible to revisit a sinful action. Maimonides noted that the laws regarding repentance are not identified or grouped in any single tractate of the Talmud. He therefore sought to reunite them and present them as a coherent set of rules in his *Mishneh Torah*. He described the process of repentance as having three stages: first confession, then regret, and finally a vow not to repeat whatever it was we did wrong. The true repentant, according to Maimonides, is someone who has the opportunity to commit the same sin once more and declines to do so. Rabbi Shlomo Wolbe explains: "The key and the beginning is the feeling one has when learning the teachings of the Sages and texts of ethical wisdom, reviewing them time and time again until they act upon a person and cause one to sense one's own personal flaws. From there one moves to the second level, which is the conquering of one's inclinations. The third level is repairing one's inclinations such that a person become joyous, and delights in the service of God." This speaks to me. The regrettably forgotten Walter Bagehot wrote at the end of the nineteenth century: "It is good to be without vices, but it is not good to be without temptations."

According to Jewish tradition, on Rosh Hashanah, God inscribes every person's fate for the coming year in the Book of Life, but he waits until Yom Kippur to seal the verdict. During that time, Jews must try to amend their behavior and seek forgiveness for any wrongs done against God and against other fellow humans. At the close of Yom Kippur, it is hoped that the transgressions of which one has truly repented have been forgiven, and one can end the day "with a merry heart." This enables the miracle of emending not the facts but the significance of the events of our past. In this healing gesture, so deeply ingrained in the work of Maimonides, I strongly believe.

Alberto Manguel
Lisbon, Yom Kippur, 2021

MAIMONIDES

Amadeo Ruiz Olmos, Statue of Maimonides, 1964, Córdoba.
The statue stands in the Jewish Quarter of the city. (Photo: Howard
Lifshitz/Wikimedia Commons, https://creativecommons.org/licenses/by/2.0)

1

The *Figure of Maimonides*

Galen's art heals only the body, but Maimonides' art
the body and the soul. With his wisdom, he could
heal the sickness of the ignorant. If the moon would
submit to his art, he could deliver her of her spots
when she shone in her fullness, cure her of her
periodic imperfections, and, at the time of her
conjunction, save her from waning.

—Ibn Sana' al-Mulk (twelfth century)

LOOK IT UP in any dictionary or history of philosophy, religion, or medicine, and the name Maimonides will appear in a
glittering swarm of epithets: "learned," "erudite," "celebrated,"
"brilliant," "prominent," "illustrious," "fabled," "the Great
Eagle," "a second Moses." But what exactly is the reason for his
extraordinary reputation?

The persecutions and hardships that Maimonides had to
endure throughout much of his life do not seem extraordinary
for the life of a medieval Jew. Even his intellectual accomplish-

ments under the difficult circumstances of his enforced peregrinations may appear to an inquiring eye, while masterly, not necessarily superior to those achieved by other men in similar conditions of exile; Dante, for instance, comes to mind. Maimonides' efforts to harmonize the various strands of philosophical inquiry from Greek and Jewish sources are not unique: in the first century BCE, Philo of Alexandria had attempted with some degree of success to interweave Greek and Jewish thought, laying the groundwork for all future intellectual commerce between Athens and Jerusalem. Perhaps one way to approach the question of Maimonides' importance is through his lifelong concentration on the laws that define the Jewish people, collectively and individually. Another is through his attempts to understand our relationship with the Creator by means of the power of reason.

Maimonides believed that the identity of the Jews lay in the Ten Commandments God gave to Moses, delivered on Mount Sinai in a speech that lacked distinct phonemes. (The great Solomon ben Isaac, popularly known as Rashi, went farther and argued that God spoke the entire set of commandments in a single incomprehensible and terrifying utterance. Another midrashic exegesis imagines God's voice mutating into seven voices and seventy languages, a Babel-like cacophony that at once addressed all the peoples of the world and was comprehensible to none.)[1] Beginning with this foundational moment of divine instruction, the Mosaic Law was variously codified, studied, interpreted, annotated, and amplified. The result was the establishment of a Written Law as set down in the book of Exodus and the other four books of the Pentateuch, to which later, progressively, were added the laws of the twenty-four books of the Jewish canon, or Tanakh. This Written Law (in Hebrew, *torah she-bikhtav*) was complemented by the Oral Law (*torah she-ba'al peh*) relayed by God to Moses, and transmitted from him and taught to the rabbinical leaders of each subsequent Jewish generation as a parallel legal code, later preserved in the Babylonian and the Palestinian Talmuds. This Oral Law was supposed to include not only the original readings of the Law but all future interpretations as well—a wealth of commentaries and explanations that included everything that had been discussed in the venerable past, everything that was being discussed in the conflictive present, and all possible interpretations in the unknowable tomorrow. This huge mass of sacred and learned material (or as much as could be discerned by rabbinical intelligence) was not laid out in any evident order or system until the second century CE, when, during the Roman occupation of Judea, a first classification was attempted by the scholarly rabbi Judah ha-Nasi (known for his intelligence as Judah the Prince) in sixty-three tractates that we now know as the Mishnah, the earliest part of the Talmud. Whether committed to writing by Judah ha-Nasi himself (as Maimonides claimed), or whether (as Rashi argued) not written out until much later, the Mishnah became the foundation of almost all successive Talmudic writings. But much remained to be done.

Besides the original Ten Commandments, many other precepts and decrees appear scattered throughout both the Hebrew Bible and the Talmud, not grouped according to subject or usage but presented in a bewildering variety of headings and contexts. Nine centuries after Judah ha-Nasi, Maimonides undertook the colossally ambitious project of extracting all the commanding precepts, of both greater and lesser importance, and arranging them in thematic groupings, interpreting and commenting on them, and translating them into logical terms to aid the willing students in their "strong desire for inquiry" that would allow them to lead sound Jewish lives.[2]

According to Maimonides, Jews were required to believe that the laws meant to govern them were divinely instated; also that their God-given gift of reason obliged them to study and try to understand these laws as thoroughly as possible, according to every individual's capabilities. Knowledge leads to the love of God, Maimonides wrote, and "the nature of one's love depends on the nature of one's knowledge."³ Perhaps the urge to question is one of the defining traits of Judaism throughout the ages. Also the urge to inquire and interpret.

Maimonides' ambition was nothing less than to define in terms as clear as possible, both for himself and for the generations to come, what it is to be a Jew. Maimonides was not a historian: though the events recorded in the Torah and the Talmud were for him indubitably true, he nevertheless viewed biblical history "through the spectacles of rabbinic legend."⁴ His answer became not a series of aphorisms or a historical summation of the sufferings of the Jewish people since the time of their exile but a lucid and atemporal system of thought that provides, even for his readers today, a rational underpinning to the open existential question Who are we, the Jews? The authors of one Maimonides biography argue emphatically that Maimonides' highest achievement was that he "taught his brethren how to think; he showed them how to live."⁵ Those words should suffice for the epitaph of any scholar deemed worthy of remembrance and praise.

One of the most bewildering aspects of Maimonides' thought is that apparent contradictions, even within one paragraph or page, do not seem to have concerned him. For Aristotle, contradictory statements cannot both be true or both be false: if one is true, the other must be false, and vice versa: unicorns exist or do not exist. Contraries, on the other hand, cannot both be true, but they can both be false: unicorns can fly, unicorns cannot fly. The political philosopher Leo Strauss has suggested a useful way of dealing with apparent contradictions in Maimonides' writings: "We may . . . establish the rule that of two contradictory statements in the *Guide* or in any other work of Maimonides, that statement which occurs least frequently, or even which occurs only once, was considered by him to be true."⁶

For the modern reader, Maimonides seems to echo Walt Whitman's future words: "Do I contradict myself? / Very well then I contradict myself, / (I am large, I contain multitudes.)"[7] Maimonides' contradictions, however, unlike Whitman's, were not self-conscious: if he saw himself in contradiction, he would have understood it as speaking different words to suit the capacity for understanding of different audiences, or finding different (even contradictory) meanings in each reading of the Law. In the words of the Talmud, "Whenever a baby searches [a breast] for milk to suckle, he finds milk in it, so too, with matters of Torah. Whenever a person meditates upon them, he finds new meaning in them," however different the meaning might appear to be every new time.[8] Every possible meaning is already there: there are no new or old versions of the sacred text. Contradictions arise from discovering different aspects of the same unchanging eternal words. To question the invariable persistence of God's word is blasphemy. Faith is not a philological exercise.

In our time, in a fiery discussion with the eminent critic Harold Bloom, who imagined literature as a constant cycle of death and reinvention of the text in the hands of each new generation, the American writer Cynthia Ozick declared that to understand poetic expression as a self-enclosed system that referred to nothing but itself was a form of idolatry. According to Ozick, in the Jewish tradition of reading the Word, "there are no latecomers." This, for Ozick, was the meaning of the words in the Passover Haggadah, "We ourselves went out from Egypt," and of the midrash that states, "All generations stood together at Sinai." Accordingly, in Jewish thought, there is "no power struggle with the original, no envy of the Creator." The idol maker, by contrast, "hopes to compete with the Creator, and schemes to invent a substitute for the Creator."[9] Maimonides made the same accusation about attempting to substitute, for the given word, new ones: "If every man were to follow after the vagaries of his heart," Maimonides writes, following the warning in Numbers 15:39, "the result would be universal ruin, ensuing from the limitations of the human intellect."[10]

Maimonides' large, multitudinous self was interested in almost everything: religion, of course, and law, but also mathematics, logic and rhetoric, astronomy, ethical behavior and social morals, politics, and the question of what can be known. Music and the visual arts did not, it seems, appeal to him, but everything else did. "There is Maimonides the defender of tradition and Maimonides the thinker who sought to reshape it, Maimonides the student of Aristotle and Maimonides the critic, Maimonides the believer and Maimonides the skeptic. Which is the real Maimonides?" asks another noted Maimonides scholar.[11]

A different puzzling aspect is the diversity of styles that Maimonides employed in his writings, a variety of discursive tones that seem to come from different persons: terse and clear in the case of the *Mishneh Torah*, for example, intended for the common reader; ambiguous and scintillatingly imaginative in that of the *Guide*, addressed to a very restricted coterie of savants; paternal and compassionate in his epistles and medical work. In his *Guide of the Perplexed* and a few other of his writings, Maimonides proposed not a closed dogmatic proclamation of Jewish identity but a multifarious one that, while based on the strict laws that appeared in the sacred texts, remained open to a panoply of interpretations by different audiences with various degrees of intellectual capacity. Only fools who willfully misread the words were dismissed. In most of his work, Maimonides was able to find a balanced relationship between the obligatory obedience to the Law and the mysterious origins of that Law, not by compounding these two but by keeping them in a continual dialogue.

Maimonides himself admits to differing in opinion from a number of established sources, and insists on giving "a different interpretation": "You will find that many among the *Sages*, and

even among the commentators, differ from [their] interpretation in regard to certain words and many notions that are set
forth by the *prophets*. How could this not be in regard to these
obscure matters?" And he concluded bravely: "Besides, I do
not oblige you to decide in favor of my interpretation. Understand the whole of his interpretation from that to which I have
drawn your attention. God knows in which of the two explanations there is a correspondence to what has been intended."[12]
Hence the richness of Maimonides' texts.

An ignorant man, Maimonides wrote, "imagines that all
that exists exists with a view to his individual stake; it is as if
there were nothing that exists except him. And if something
happens to him that is contrary to what he wishes, he makes the
trenchant judgment that all that exists is an evil. However, if
man considered and represented to himself that which exists
and knew the smallness of his part in it, the truth would become clear and manifest to him."[13] Perhaps it is this clear intellectual honesty, backed by a prodigious learning, that makes
Maimonides "the soundest of the Hebrew Rabbins" for John
Donne, and one of the best-loved seekers of the truth.[14]

I undertook this book with great awareness of my innocence in matters religious, halakhic, and medical, and perfectly
ignorant of Arabic and Hebrew. My only excuse is a keen interest in Maimonides' quest to understand what lies beyond words,
and how this knowledge can be put in service of "the Greater
Good." I realize that I tread in the footsteps of hundreds of
great scholars who have analyzed and discussed, with much intelligence and perception, Maimonides' writings throughout
the centuries and up to this day. I can claim no more than the
doubtful virtues of a curious reader.

2

Al-Andalus

Thus were the sweet days now past
When profiting of Fate's slumber
We behaved as thieves of pleasure.

—Ibn Zaydun (eleventh century)

MAIMONIDES HAS MANY NAMES. In the Arab world he is known as Musa ibn 'Ubayd Allah the Israelite from Córdoba, in the Jewish as Ha-Moreh (teacher) or Ha-Rav ha-Moreh, following the Hebrew title of his best-known work, *The Guide of the Perplexed* or *Moreh Nevukhim*. And after his death, he was called by his devoted admirers by the acronym Rambam (RaMBaM) or Rabbeinu, "Our Master Moshe ben Maimon." The life story of Maimonides has a certain epic, even mythical quality, and legends and fantastic tales about his miraculous powers circulated long before and long after his death.

Some have the peculiar flavor of the *Arabian Nights.* One of the legends takes place during his sojourn in Egypt and tells of a test that the sultan imposed on Maimonides and a jealous rival. The rival had said that he could prove that Maimonides had concocted an infamous plot to poison the sultan. Since (according to the rival) everyone knew that a deadly poison could be made harmless by imbibing one stronger, the sultan should order both him and Maimonides to prepare the strongest poison imaginable, with the understanding that if the sultan were served poisoned food, all he would have to do would be to take the strongest poison, and his life would be saved. The sultan agreed. Maimonides was ordered to drink his rival's concoction, and then, as an antidote, the one he himself had prepared. Maimonides did so with no apparent ill effects. But when his rival drank Maimonides' poison and then his own, he collapsed in agony and quickly expired. Maimonides then explained to the sultan what had happened. "My rival knew that I could prepare a stronger poison than he could, so he thought of a cunning plan: he would take a slow poison before coming to the Palace, and bring with him a harmless solution. By drinking what he thought would be my stronger poison, he would be cured of the less lethal concoction he had taken at home. He would then drink his own harmless mixture and all would be well, while I, in the meantime, would drink his mixture followed by my own strong poison, and thus, he believed, I would die by my own hand." "The treacherous dog!" the sultan cried. "But what really happened?" "Your majesty," Maimonides answered. "Because I suspected this trickery, I also prepared a harmless mixture."[1]

Another story tells of Maimonides' courteous kindness to all, famous scholars and common folk alike. Every Sabbath, Maimonides is known to have invited guests—especially the impoverished—to his house. One evening, Maimonides offered his guest the honor of reciting kiddush, the ceremonial blessing over the wine. But at that moment, certainly due to his nervousness, the visitor inadvertently caused his goblet to tip over and the wine spilled on Maimonides' tablecloth. Aware of his guest's distress, Maimonides immediately poured himself another goblet and jostled the table intentionally, upsetting his own goblet and also spilling the wine. He then stood up and said, "It seems to me that the floor here isn't very level."[2]

One of the legends highlights the keen intellectual achievements of Maimonides in his youth by alluding to the rumor that his mother was a common butcher's daughter whom Maimonides' father, Maimon ben Yosef, was instructed in a dream to marry. That was the reason, it was said, that his father called him "butcher's son" when the boy would not apply himself to his studies.[3] (A similar legend was associated with the boy Shakespeare, lending the future author of *Macbeth* the role of a butcher's apprentice in Stratford.)[4]

Other tales belong to the realm of hagiography. After his death, it is said that Maimonides' body was placed for a week in a small shrine somewhere in the region of Acre, where as a young man he used to study at night and heal strangers during the day. The body was then taken to the western shore of the Sea of Galilee for burial in Tiberias. On the way, a group of Bedouins who were about to attack the funeral procession suddenly realized that the body being carried was that of the man who in the past had attended to them and their families for free. Instead of robbing the mourners, they formed a guard of honor around the body to ensure that the procession could proceed unharmed. Joseph ben Isaac Sambari, a Jewish-Egyptian traveler of the seventeenth century, added to the story that the mourners absent-mindedly left behind one of the Master's toes. During the night, one of the carriers had a dream in which an old man appeared and reproved him for his negligence. The mourner returned, recovered the missing toe, and devotedly buried it with the rest of the body.[5]

Even as recently as the early twentieth century, the magical powers attributed to Maimonides were still alive. In 1935, when King Fuad I of Egypt became seriously ill, the loyal inhabitants of the Jewish Quarter of Cairo borrowed some of the monarch's clothes, took them to the prayer room in Maimonides' synagogue, and kept them there for a week, after which, it was said, "the king's health miraculously improved."[6]

If the spiritual portrait of the enlightened scholar sometimes strays from the field of historically proven facts, the physical image of Maimonides is just as elusive, as behooves an almost legendary figure. The only more-or-less trustworthy likeness we have of him is the reproduction of a medallion in an eighteenth-century multi-volume encyclopedia on the subject of antiquities, the *Thesaurus Antiquitatum Sacrarum* (1744–1769) printed by Blasius Ugolinus in Venice. The portrait depicts a turbaned, bearded man with an anachronistic medal hanging from his neck. Whether or not a true depiction of Moses Maimonides, it was copied many times, and is the one that appears today in the majority of books on the Rambam.[7]

Moses ben Maimon, or simply Maimonides, as he is known to us today, was born in Córdoba, in the heart of al-Andalus, the realm of Arabic Spain the Jews called Sepharad, on Passover Eve, 30 March 1138 (4898 in the Jewish calendar) reportedly at 1:00 in the afternoon.[8] Throughout his life, Maimonides considered Sepharad his spiritual home and referred often to his Sephardic roots. Medieval Sepharad nourished great Jewish poets such as Solomon ibn Gabirol and Judah ha-Levi, as well as scholars such as Avraham ben Meir ibn Ezra, and it still, in Maimonides' time, retained much of the glory of its former days. Maimonides spent the first thirteen years of his life in Córdoba before being forced with his family into a long, erratic exile, first to other regions of Spain, then to North Africa and Palestine. Finally, in 1165, Maimonides settled in Egypt, in what was nine years later to become Saladin's Cairo, where he died, universally mourned, in 1204. These are the bare chronological facts.

The Arabs had arrived in the Iberian peninsula in 710. The first wave of settlers were Berber and Arab tribes from North

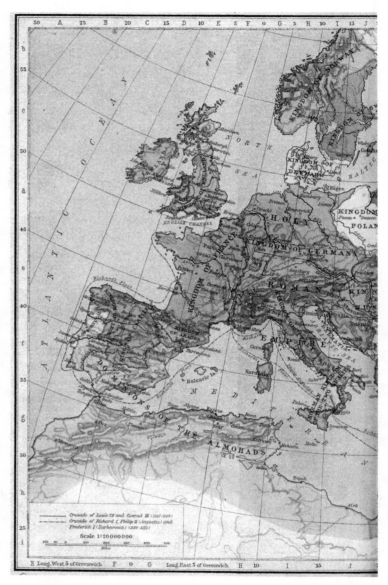

Map of Europe and the Mediterranean lands about 1190.
From William R. Shepherd, *The Historical Atlas* (1926), Perry-Castañeda
Library Map Collection, University of Texas Libraries. (Photo: Perry-
Castañeda Library Map Collection, University of Texas Libraries)

Guelf, Hohenstaufen and Ascanian domains
in Germany about 1176

Guelf   Hohenstaufen   Ascanian

Scale 1:15 000 000

*The dark coloring indicates hereditary or imperial domains;
light coloring, feudal territories; and border coloring, suzerainty.*

Africa; soon they were joined by militia from Syria, supporters of the Umayyad dynasty. With a firm hand, the Umayyads took hold of their new province in the westernmost region of Europe and ruled there for almost three hundred years. Some two centuries after the first settlements, in 912, the young emir 'Abd al-Rahman III ascended to the Umayyad throne and ten years later adopted the title of caliph, thereby placing what had until then been the emirate of Córdoba on a par with the Abbasid caliphate of Baghdad and the Shiite caliphate of Tunis. What is known as the Golden Age of al-Andalus—an unprecedented flowering of the arts, letters, commerce, and political power—had begun.

During the Umayyad rule, the Jews of Sepharad found unexpected prosperity, both commercial and cultural, and a measured amount of religious and intellectual freedom. Earlier, under the domination of the Visigoth Catholic rulers, the Jews of Spain had been relegated to the lowest social stratum; now the Umayyads decreed that the Jews, as People of the Book, came under the category of *dhimmi*, "protected," a status sometimes granted to non-Muslims living in a Muslim country. The Qur'an (29:46) states that "[Believers] argue only in the best way with the People of the Book, except with those of them who act unjustly. Say, 'We believe in what was revealed to us and in what was revealed to you; our God and your God is one [and the same]; we are devoted to Him.'" The Jews were accordingly authorized to take part in the civilian life of the community and, most important, had their religious customs guaranteed. Quickly the Jews acquired a reputation as skillful administrators and medical doctors, and also as adroit merchants dealing in perfumes, furs, and slaves.

Jewish commerce had played an important role in the slave trade since the eighth century across Europe and the Mediterranean. Under 'Abd al-Rahman, the slave trade flourished. In Maimonides' time, Córdoba alone had over thirteen thousand slaves, of which a fourth labored in the royal country palace of Madinat al-Zahra.[9] Maimonides in his later years would enjoin compassionate treatment for slaves: "All the *commandments* we have enumerated in *Laws concerning Slaves* are all of them imbued with pity and benevolence for the weak," he writes, noting that a slave who runs away from a harsh master must not be returned to that master; more, "It is not even enough to protect those who seek your protection, for you are under another obligation toward him: you must consider his interests, be beneficent toward him, and not pain his heart by speech."[10]

The Jews, obliged to be resourceful, began to profit from the new society into which they were gradually integrated, developing an Arab-Jewish culture of their own. "In many respects," notes the scholar María Rosa Menocal, "the flourishing of Jewish culture went hand in hand with the heyday of Arabic, particularly secular Arabic, culture. In great measure, both cultural zeniths were due to the same liberalism and tolerance, and ultimately they would both be destroyed by the same intolerance." For us today, witnessing a resurgence of Islamophobia and anti-Semitism, this last observation is of essential importance.[11]

Córdoba in the tenth century had become, in the words of the tenth-century Saxon scholar Hroswitha, "the ornament of the world."[12] The city ramparts, built on Roman remains, had 13 gates and 132 towers. There were 1,600 mosques, 900 public baths, 80,000 shops, over 60,000 mansions for the nobility and the military commanders, and close to a quarter-million homes for the rest of the population.[13]

The administration of the city improved on the traditional Abbasid, Byzantine, and Persian governmental systems. Power was maintained by what was then the largest fleet in the world, coupled with a powerful army. Several arms workshops in the proximity of Córdoba produced, among other weapons, one thousand bows and twenty thousand arrows a month. The central government in Córdoba itself was linked to the provinces by a well-policed network of roads and an efficient postal service that employed messenger pigeons.[14] What the poet Peter Cole calls "a near-alphabet of crops" were imported and flourished in the Andalusian soil: "apricots, artichokes, bananas, carrots, eggplants, figs, hard wheat, lemons, oranges, parsnips, peaches, pomegranates, rice, saffron, spinach, sugarcane, and watermelon."[15]

With a population of perhaps half a million, Córdoba overtook Constantinople as the largest and most prosperous city in Europe, becoming at the same time one of the leading intellectual centers, on par with Baghdad and Toledo. Muslims and non-Muslims alike came from abroad to study in its famous libraries and universities, taking back to their native lands the knowledge they had acquired in Córdoba. In the mid-tenth century, under al-Hakam II, Córdoba's central library had held over four hundred thousand volumes, and smaller private and public libraries were known to contain numerous invaluable treasures. Two centuries later, this was still the case. The book market employed over seventy copyists for the Qur'an alone, many of whom were women, who also worked as librarians, teachers, doctors, and lawyers.[16]

A fair section of the book market was in the hands of Jews. Moses ibn Ezra, a distinguished poet from Granada, was to remark that the skill of the Córdoba Jews to learn the Arab language and customs was nothing short of miraculous. "They became excellent scholars in their various scientific disciplines. . . . But there where the imitation became most perfect was in the art of poetry, because they assimilated their methods and were very sensitive to their marvels."[17] Judeo-Arabic poetry was to lay the foundations for the development of Spanish and Portuguese poetry that flourished centuries later. The cadences and themes of the poets of al-Andalus still echo through the Spanish poets of today.

The dwindling Christian community, known as Mozarabs, also adopted some of the features of the dominant Arab culture while at the same time attempting to remain unobtrusively faithful to their religion. But the Christians soon felt that this middle ground was impossible to maintain, and were faced with two painful options: convert to Islam or depart into exile.

The Jews too would soon be confronted with this grave choice. But even after the tolerant Umayyad regime, during Maimonides' adolescence under the Almoravids, Jewish scholars were still able to pursue their studies: they continued to write and communicate daily in Arabic, they joined the educated Arab elite and embraced Arabic thought with intellectual passion. With more success than the Mozarabs, they also managed to preserve their rituals and liturgy.

The two cultures, Islamic and Jewish, were seen as tenuously complementary and remained respectful of one another, each pursuing the commandments of its own faith. Perhaps the fact that the Jewish community was in the minority in Arab al-Andalus made its members more sensitive to the ideas that flourished in the world of their rulers. And yet Maimonides' remarkable achievements lie less in his efforts to integrate the teachings of the different cultures he experienced than in the vast scope and unusual precision of the cultural synthesis he reached in his work.

In al-Andalus, the Arabic and Hebrew tongues commingled. Maimonides, for example, after ruling that for the Jews daily prayers were mandatory, borrowed an image from the Qur'an to explain that the God to whom they prayed was like a fire. Rather than referring to the burning bush in Exodus, Maimonides cited the Qur'anic properties of fire: properties of action, not identity. Fire can soften wax, harden clay, blacken sugar, and whiten other things, but fire is not soft, hard, black, or white: fire simply has these effects on the various things put in contact with it.[18] Not only images taken from the other culture took root in the writings of both communities: terms and expressions in one language would serve to communicate concepts and procedures that lacked a proper name in the other. Describing this linguistic interweaving evident, for instance, in the recitation of Hebrew prayers, Maimonides observed, "When anyone of them [the Jews] prayed in Hebrew, he was unable adequately to express his needs or recount the praises of God, without mixing Hebrew with other languages."[19] The curse of Babel had little effect in al-Andalus.

"Let a person use an expensive goblet one day and let it break tomorrow" is the Talmudic version of "carpe diem."[20] The golden days of Sepharad did not last. The Córdoba caliphate effectively collapsed during the civil war that broke out between 1009 and 1013, and was finally abolished in 1031. Al-Andalus became divided into a number of small *taifas*, or factions, governed by weak and ineffective kinglets, "breaking the necklace and scattering the pearls" as one Arab writer put it.[21] What had been one of the most urbane societies in the world now became increasingly threatened by the Christian armies from the North, especially the Castilians led by King Alfonso VI. Seeking protection from these attacks, the people of al-Andalus appealed to the Almoravids across the sea, a Berber tribe from the Sahara who had succeeded in establishing a powerful empire in Morocco. In response to their plea, the Almoravids crossed over from North Africa, kept the Christian legions at bay, deposed the remaining Umayyad rulers, and in 1086 set al-Andalus under their rule.

In spite of enduring a stricter, less tolerant system of Islamic government than when under the Umayyads, Córdoba under the Almoravids remained for at least another century an important multicultural center that allowed the intellectual exchange between Muslims and Jews to continue, for a time at least. Owing to the efforts of Arab philosophers and scientists such as Al-Zahrawi (Latinized as Abulcasis) and Ibn Rushd

(Averroës), who continued to translate and comment on the works of the ancient Greeks (Aristotle especially, but Plato and Neoplatonists like Plotinus in the third century CE as well), both Arabs and Jews were able to learn from the ancient masters; write memorable poetry, remarkable medical handbooks, and profound philosophical treatises; and share ideas and scientific discoveries. Then the Almohads arrived.

The Almohads were a people originally from the northwest of Africa who followed the teachings of the Sunni master Al-Ghazali, widely considered a *mujaddid*, a defender of the true faith who is deemed to appear once every hundred years to strengthen the rule of Islam. In light of Al-Ghazali's teachings, and believing that dangerous laxity had infected the religious life of al-Andalus, the Almohads decided to put an end to the Almoravid rule. They quickly set up harsh religious strictures, making life very difficult for the Jewish community. A Moroccan chronicler of the time noted that under Almohad rule, the dhimma protocol set up by the Umayyads was all but abolished: Jews were required to wear distinctive clothing, Jewish inheritances were confiscated, and Jewish children were sometimes removed from their parents' care and raised as Muslims, following an ancient Islamic saying that declares that "every child is by nature a Muslim."[22] Already in 1113, the Almohad leader Ibn Tumart proclaimed that all the Jews should be obliged to abandon their religion. "Come, let us cut them off from being a nation," he announced, "so that the name of Israel may be no more in remembrance!"[23]

A few decades later, under Prince 'Abd al-Mu'min, the second Almohad monarch to ascend to the throne in North Africa, further laws were enforced throughout the region that stipulated that non-Muslims would not be allowed in the Almohad states. The moderate freedom that the Jews had enjoyed in al-Andalus was finally forfeited. This led Maimonides in later years to declare that as regarded the Almohads, "there never came against Israel a more inimical nation," even worse than that of the Christians.[24]

In 1147, the Almohads crossed the Straits of Gibraltar; a year later, they entered Córdoba. The local population surrendered to the invaders for fear of a worse fate: falling into the hands of the still threatening Christian hosts in the North. Synagogues and churches were torn down or changed into mosques, and both Jews and Mozarabs were forced to choose between immediate conversion to Islam and exile. Many—both Jews and Christians—agreed to convert while secretly continuing the observance of their own religion. Others chose to leave. Maimon ben Yosef decided to take his family out of Córdoba to a safer home. By then, the Maimonides family consisted of the father, his second wife, the young Moses, one-year-old David, and two or three daughters, of whom little is known except the name of the youngest, Miriam.

Maimon ben Yosef was descended from a long line of notable scholars whose names Maimonides himself lists in the colophon of his *Commentary on the Mishnah.* "I am Moses, son of Rabbi Maimon, son of the scholar Josef, son of Rabbi Isaac, son of Rabbi Josef, son of Rabbi Abdias, son of Rabbi Solomon, son of Rabbi Abdias. May the memory of these holy men bring blessings on us!"[25] The boy received rabbinical instruction in both Hebrew and Arabic from his scholarly father and was introduced to some of the most notable Arab scholars active in Córdoba at the time in order to cultivate what the Andalusians called *adab,* "cultural refinement." Not a negligible stimulus to a mind that even then was beginning to conceive the astonishingly ambitious projects of later years.

3

North Africa and Palestine

A palm tree I beheld in Ar-Rusafa
Far in the West, far from the palm-tree land:
I said to it: You, like myself, are far away, in a strange
　　land;
How long have I been far away from my people!
You grew up in a land where you are a stranger,
And like myself, are living in the farthest corner of
　　the earth:
May the morning clouds refresh you at this distance,
And may abundant rains comfort you forever!

　　　—'Abd al-Rahman I (eighth century)

IT IS DURING ONE'S CHILDHOOD that the landscapes of adult
dreams are fashioned. The exquisite architecture of Córdoba
with its lacework of stone and its patios alive with running
water, the pink hills and green orchards encircling the city, the
bustling and colorful souk under whose canopies everything in
the world was traded, the studious quiet of the academies and

21

libraries where the readers' concentration was accompanied by the cadences of Talmudic and Qur'anic recitations, the spicy-sweet smells rising from the markets and orange groves—all these became the rich sensorial background against which Maimonides' intellect developed. Being forced to leave it must have been for the young Maimonides a heart-wrenching bereavement. Four centuries later, Ricote, Sancho Panza's neighbor, exiled from his native Spain because of his Arab blood, would put into words what the adolescent Maimonides must have felt: "Wherever we find ourselves, we weep for Spain, since there we were born and since there is our natural homeland."[1]

The Maimonides family traveled first to Almería, where they stayed for nine years until the Almohad army invaded that city as well. Forced to flee once again, they may have lived in Seville for a time, where the young Maimonides might have met the "very proficient" Arab astronomers mentioned later in his *Guide*.[2]

Since the Peninsula afforded the family no security, in 1160 they decided to cross over to North Africa and settle in Morocco, in the city of Fez, whose ancient Arabic architecture, brought over to the Peninsula centuries earlier by the first Islamic settlers, now seemed to Maimonides a sad imitation of the houses and gardens of his beloved Córdoba. As a true son of Sepharad, Maimonides felt that North Africa, in spite of its undoubtedly Arabic character, was utterly foreign to him, simply because it was not his homeland. Maimonides was now in his twenty-second year, and his scholarly gifts were beginning to be recognized among the intellectual elite.

Fez proved not to be a good choice. A century and a half earlier, in 1033, the forces of the Banu Ifran, a Zenata Berber tribe from the region, had conquered the city and attacked the Jewish population, killing over six thousand Jews. They looted Jewish belongings and took Jewish women as slaves. Only when, years later, another Berber tribe, the Almohads, invaded Fez and forced the Banu Ifran to flee the city was the Jewish population able to reestablish itself with some measure of security. Nevertheless, it seems strange that, with the memory of the massacre still obviously present in the ritual recital of the Yizkor (Remember) prayer for the ancestral dead, Maimon ben Yosef would choose Fez as a haven for his family.

The Almohads had wanted to transform Fez into a powerful social center, effectively diminishing its rural character. They forcibly transported a number of Arab families from al-Andalus to Fez, so that between 1170 and 1180 Fez's population grew to an estimated two hundred thousand, making it one of the most important cities in North Africa. Perhaps it was the newly acquired prestige of the city that attracted Maimon ben Yosef, as well as the fact that, in spite of the intolerance, the Jewish community of Fez had persisted and even prospered.

The Almohads continued to tighten the restrictions against the Jews, and the Maimonides family was probably forced to conduct its public business under the guise of Muslims. Perhaps the chaos of enforced exile led Maimonides to study in depth the laws in the holy books, trying to satisfy a need for balance in an unbalanced world, to counterpoise the social confusion with a learned order and a structured set of rules for a virtuous and good life. Whatever the reason behind his scholarly decision, the young Maimonides' reputation in the field of Jewish law kept growing. This rendered him suspicious in the eyes of the Islamic authorities, who began to doubt his veritable religious inclination. The thirteenth-century physician Ibn Abi Usaybi'a noted, "It has been said that Maimonides converted to Islam in the West [*maghrib*], that he learned the Quran by heart, and that he occupied himself with Muslim law." Though unproven, none of this seems unlikely, if only as a strategy of survival. Years later, in answer to a question on apostasy, Maimonides advocated toleration for the "appearance" of conversion when one's life was threatened, and even ruled that one who submitted to death when not obligated to do so committed a capital offense.[3] Furthermore, it does not seem surprising that someone who took such interest in the law, albeit Jewish, and served as an apprentice in a rabbinical court in Fez should also wish to study the religious laws of Islam and, if necessary, pretend to follow them.

The American scholar Ammiel Alcalay has argued that those "categorized as 'others' must constantly remain alert to the implications and contexts of both exclusion *and* inclusion. They must continually devise new ways of thinking and acting, speaking and keeping silent, to avoid fulfilling the sterile role of either 'heroic artist' or 'unspoiled native.'"[4] So it was with Maimonides. A voracious searcher after knowledge, Maimonides was at the time also studying medicine, mathematics, and astronomy, as well as Talmudic and midrashic commentaries (the latter comprising both legal and imaginative exegesis), which he trained himself to learn by heart. In his Córdoba childhood, following the educational precepts of the time, Maimonides would have been taught to memorize not only the Torah but also the Mishnah and large portions of the Talmud in order to be able to advance in his studies, since it was said that one could memorize without understanding, but that understanding without memorizing was impossible.[5]

While in Fez, because of an anonymous accusation, Maimonides was charged with the crime of having forsworn the Islamic faith. He was saved from capital punishment by the intercession of the poet and theologian Abu al-'Arab al-Mu'ishah, who had befriended him upon arrival. But these tribulations proved once again too much for the family, and in 1165, five years after their arrival, they took to the road once more, this time bound for Palestine.

Palestine proved no different. On 23 May 1165 the Maimonides family arrived in Acre; then, after a time, they traveled on to Jerusalem. According to a note in a commentary by Maimonides on the Talmudic tractate *Rosh Hashanah*, in the autumn of 1165 Maimonides "left Acre to go up to Jerusalem, with the attendant danger; I entered the great holy house and prayed in it."[6] The prophet Isaiah had said that "instruction shall come forth from Zion, The Word of the LORD from Jerusalem"(Isaiah 2:3). Maimonides felt that he had come to the place from which the Law of God had issued (as Isaiah had metonymically phrased it). And yet the Holy City was not for him.

Jerusalem at the time was governed by Amalric, count of Jaffa, only brother of King Baldwin III, who had been crowned three years earlier by the patriarch of Jerusalem. Under Amalric, Jews and Muslims, as well as Eastern Orthodox Christians, had virtually no rights in the Christian kingdom of Palestine and were deemed essentially the property of the crusader lord who owned the land on which they settled. This intolerance for their religious practices, however, seems to have been no worse than what existed elsewhere in the Christian Middle East, an intolerance justified by the crusaders' motto *Deus lo vult*, "God wills this."[7]

There are no reliable documents attesting to the exact dates of the Maimonides family's peregrinations in Palestine. The only certainty is that in the same year of their arrival in Jerusalem, they left again, this time for Egypt.

4

Egypt

Perish not through despair: only be patient.

—"Ode of Imru al-Qais" in *The Mu'allaqat*
(eighth century)

In Egypt, the Maimonides family took up residence in Fustat, as Old Cairo was known. Founded in 641, Fustat became the first Islamic capital of Egypt until New Cairo (al-Qahira) was built adjacent to it at the end of the tenth century. It nevertheless remained an important commercial center, dealing in glass, ceramics, and paper, with a busy port that attracted travelers from around the world. "The city itself was densely populated with dark, narrow streets wriggling between brick tenement blocks up to seven storeys high. Public hygiene was legendarily terrible, with latrines that drained directly into the Nile, which happened to be the main water supply, polluting it so badly that the fish died and putrefied."[1] Fustat was certainly not Córdoba.

In Fustat, Maimonides married the daughter of Mishael ben Yeshayahu Halevi—her own name has not come down to

OLD CAIRO (FOSTÂT).

Fustat (Fostât; Old Cairo). From S. Rappoport, *History of Egypt from 330 B.C. to the Present Time*, 12 vols. (London: Grolier Society, 1904), vol. II, chap. 3.

us. Of their children (their exact number is not recorded), only Avraham survived into adulthood and became a talented scholar who succeeded his father as court physician at the age of eighteen. Avraham was a fervent defender of his father's halakhic writings and, as a reformer in his own right and in contrast to his father's traditionalism, he attempted to introduce Sufi elements into the ancestral Jewish rituals of his community. His best-known work, the *Kifayat al-Abidin* (Guide for the Pious), of which only fragments have survived, argues for Jews to embrace a lifelong devout attitude to interiorize the practices of their faith, strengthening it through performance and ritual. After Maimonides' death, Avraham attempted "the purification of Jewish monotheism after the model of Islam," which led to the establishment of the foremost spiritual movement among medieval Egyptian Jews, known as the *Hasidut* or Pietism.[2]

But a new series of misfortunes awaited Maimonides in Egypt. First his father died, leaving the family in deep mourning. Then, sometime between 1169 and 1177, his brother David, who had supported the family by trading in precious stones, boarded, against Maimonides' advice, a ship bound for India, which sank before reaching its destination. These two deaths plunged Maimonides into a profound depression that lasted for over a year, and which he diagnosed himself as "a medical condition." Maimonides wrote about his experience: "When a man with a powerful frame, a sonorous voice, and a radiant complexion hears sudden news that greatly afflicts him, one can see his face turning pale, the glow dimming, the body hunching, the voice faltering, and when he tries with all his might to raise his voice, he is unable to do so, his strength is weakened. Indeed, he often trembles with feebleness, his pulse slows down, his eyes move back in their sockets. His eyelids grow so heavy that he cannot move them, his body becomes cold, and his appetite vanishes."[3]

Since antiquity, depression (under the various names of melancholia, black bile, and, later, acidia) was recognized as a psychosomatic state that had both salutary and noxious aspects. Aristotle, in one of the "problems" attributed to him (but collected sometime between the third century BCE and the sixth century CE) asked why melancholy and genius are so often associated.[4] Aretheus of Capodocea, in the first century CE, noted that many melancholics, if they were cultured men, showed a miraculous disposition to discourse on philosophy, astronomy, and poetry, while those who were good with their hands could produce marvels of carpentry and pottery.[5] The Arab physician Al-Razi, in the ninth century, described the divinatory capacity of some of his patients afflicted by melancholy, and noted that they were prone to having prophetic visions, many times proven to be true.[6]

To counter a depression such as this, Maimonides recommended tending to the five senses "for the purpose of quickening the soul." Hearing was to be nourished "by listening to stringed and reed-pipe music," seeing "by gazing at beautiful pictures," smelling "by strolling through beautiful gardens," feeling "by wearing fine raiment," and tasting "by eating highly seasoned delicacies." Such things, Maimonides judged, "are not to be considered immoral nor unnecessary."[7] These recommendations give us a rare glimpse into the private man and allow the question of whether, under the stern guise of his role as adviser and legislator, Maimonides could enjoy good food and the smell of jasmine in a garden for their own sake. Cairo was not Córdoba, but it would do. Intellectual pursuits, both religious and scientific, he tells us, were of help to lift a little the dark clouds.

However, the sense of mourning for his father and brother lingered on for many years, perhaps until the end of his life. In a letter of 1185, answering a judge from Acre whom the family had befriended when in Palestine, and who had complained of not having had news from them since their departure decades earlier, Maimonides explained:

> A few months after we departed from [Palestine], my father and master died (may the memory of the righteous be a blessing). Letters of condolences arrived from the furthest west

and from the land of Edom. . . . Furthermore, I suffered many well-known calamities in Egypt, including sickness, financial loss and the attempt by informers to have me killed.

The worst disaster that struck me of late, worse than anything I had ever experienced from the time I was born until this day, was the demise of that upright man (may the memory of the righteous be a blessing), who drowned in the Indian Ocean while in possession of much money belonging to me, to him and to others, leaving a young daughter and his widow in my care. For about a year from the day the evil tidings reached me I remained prostrate in bed with a severe inflammation, fever and mental confusion, and well nigh perished.

From then until this day, that is about eight years, I have been in a state of disconsolate mourning. How can I be consoled? For he was my son; he grew up upon my knees; he was my brother, my pupil. It was he who did business in the marketplace, earning a livelihood, while I dwelled in security. He had a ready grasp of the Talmud and a superb mastery of grammar. My only joy was to see him. "The sun has set on all joy." [Isa. 24:11.] For he has gone on to eternal life, leaving me dismayed in a foreign land. Whenever I see his handwriting or one of his books my heart is churned inside me and my sorrow is rekindled. . . .] And were it not for the Torah, which is my delight, and for scientific matters, which let me forget my sorrow, "I would have perished in my affliction" [Ps. 119:92].[8]

Forcing himself to step out of the depression in order to confront the loss of the family business and find other ways of procuring an income, but judging it a sin to make money from religious teaching, Maimonides turned to medicine as a means of livelihood. Maimonides regarded the body and the spirit as one in God's creation and argued that it was essential to awaken and instruct both. Maimonides was convinced that the study of the Torah should be complemented by the study of nature it-

self, God's other book, in which no page remained unturned for
long, and that empirical scientific inquiry allows us the knowledge of our world and our changing physical self. "No form
remains constantly in it, for it perpetually puts off one form
and puts on another," Maimonides wrote.[9] He was describing
not only the quality of the mutable universe that he endeavored
to understand but also his own condition as a Jewish exile,
condemned to seemingly endless wandering and displacement,
"while my mind was troubled, and amid divinely ordained exiles,
on journeys by land and tossed on the tempests of the sea."[10]

The first troubled Egyptian years were intensely produc-
tive, because Maimonides managed to find, even in the midst
of a host of constraints, misfortunes, and sufferings, the spiritual and intellectual strength to keep on working. During this
time, Maimonides produced a large number of writings of which
the most important is without doubt his masterwork, written
in Arabic: the *Dalalat al-Ḥa'iri*, known in Hebrew as *Moreh
Nevukhim* and in English as *The Guide of the Perplexed*. The
Guide became a fundamental text of medieval philosophical inquiry, not only for Jewish scholars but also as an inspiration for
both Muslim and Christian thinkers.

After several years of practicing medicine in Fustat, Maimonides had firmly established his reputation as a medical doctor. The majority of his medical works were translated from
Judeo-Arabic into Hebrew and Latin, and as his fame grew, so
did his professional obligations. He worked indefatigably. And
yet, even after becoming the untitled head of the Jewish community in Egypt, he continued to refuse to accept remunera-
tion for his services, in accordance with his ethical principles
and the dictates of the Talmud: "Just as I [Moshe] [teach for]
free so too you [must teach for] free."[11] Aware of Maimonides'
reputation, Sultan Saladin's vizier, Al-Kadi al-Fadil al-Baisami,
made him his personal physician and recommended Maimonides to the royal family.

Tomb of Maimonides, Tiberias, Israel. (Photo: Deror_avi/Wikimedia
Commons, https://creativecommons.org/licenses/by-sa/4.0)

Certain scholars have suggested that "the King of the Franks
in Ascalon" (that is, England's Richard I) offered Maimonides a
similar position, which Maimonides refused.[12] Sir Walter Scott,
in his 1825 romance *The Talisman*, imagines Saladin sending
to his sick rival King Richard his personal Moorish physician,
Adonbec el Hakim: modern editors have suggested that under
that name, Scott meant to portray Maimonides.[13] Though the
Richard story persists now only in Scott's fiction, it nevertheless
shows the extent of Maimonides' fame. Like Saladin, Richard
could have very well wished to have the renowned physician at
his bedside. Saladin was born in the same year as Maimonides.
In 1193, preceding Maimonides by thirteen years, Saladin died
and was succeeded by one of his seventeen sons, al-Muzaffar
Umar ibn Nur Al-Din. Maimonides' workload increased to the
breaking point.

Maimonides himself died in Fustat in 1204, probably from
exhaustion. He was sixty-six years old. Jews around the world

grieved for their loss, and in Fustat itself, both Jews and Arabs went into a three-day public mourning, while in Jerusalem, the rabbinical authorities proclaimed a general fast. Maimonides' body was taken to Tiberias on the Sea of Galilee, where his tomb quickly became a place of pilgrimage. His books have ever since been a cornerstone of Jewish thought and Jewish identity, and his medical knowledge has secured for him a distinguished place in the history of medicine.

5

------◆·◆·◆------

Maimonides the Physician

BY THE TENTH CENTURY, the arts of medicine were flourishing in the Arab world. Scholars such as the Jewish doctor
Isaac Israeli ben Solomon, author of the *Kitab al-Istiḳat* (Book
of the Elements, following the teachings of Aristotle), and the
Persian Ali ibn al-Abbas, author of the *Kitab al-Maliki* (Complete Book of the Medical Art), composed individual treatises
on fevers, pharmaceutical drugs, digestive ailments, and res-
piratory diseases. Others, among them Hunayn ibn Ishaq, a
Christian medical scholar fluent not only in Arabic and Greek
but also in Syriac and Persian who became known in the West
as Johannitius and in the East as "the Sheikh of Translators,"
rendered into Arabic many of the works of the classical Greek
physicians, principally Galen and Hippocrates, with such precision that it was said that "they needed no corrections."[1] Two
centuries later, exploring the libraries open to him in his several ports of call, Maimonides must have studied the writings

Primus Aui. canon.

Auicēne medicoɀ principis canonū Liber: vna
cūlucidiſſima Gētilis Fulgi. erpoſitione: qui
merito eſt Speculatoɀ appellatus.
Additis annotationibus oium auctoɀitatum ɀ
priſcoɀ ɀ recentioɀ auctoɀ: propɀijs locis fm
propɀia eoɀuɀ cap. vel cōmenta: pulchɀo etiaɀ
indice eɀoɀnatus: qui fm capituloɀum nume-
rum: dubioɀum oɀdinem oſtendit.

Nuper ſollerti cura coɀrectus: ab infinitiſqɀ fe-
re erroɀibus emēdatus: ɀ nouiter in edi-
bus heredū Octauiani Scoti ac
socioɀ: omni cum dilige-
tia impɀeſſus.

First [and Second] Avicenna *Canon* with commentary by Gentile da Foligno,
published in 1520 in Venice. Illustration shows Avicenna (*left*) as "Princeps
Abinsceni" and (*right*) Gentile da Foligno. (© Wellcome Collection)

of these scholars, as well as the great medical compilations of Al-Razi, Avicenna's *Canon*, and Abulcasis's *Chirurgia* that were available at the time.

In Christian Europe, thanks to the translations of most of these texts into Latin, Western physicians became convinced that medicine should be studied as a rational system with close ties to philosophy, grounded in logic and the object of methodical investigation: their Jewish and Arab colleagues were well aware of this long before.[2] "In the sciences," Avicenna, the great tenth-century Persian polymath, wrote, "no knowledge is acquired save through the study of its causes and beginnings. . . . One may say that medicine is divided into theoretical and practical, and I have made it all theoretical by saying it is a science."[3] Maimonides could have written these exact words.

For Maimonides, the science of medicine, other than a means of earning a living, was an essential and valid way of achieving the Aristotelian eudaemonia: that is to say, the best conditions possible for a happy, virtuous, and meaningful life. "The art of medicine," he wrote, "plays a very important role in acquiring both ethical knowledge and the knowledge of God, that is, the attainment of true *eudaemonia*. The study of medicine is a valid form of divine worship. . . . Through medicine we calibrate our bodily actions, actions that allow the body to become an instrument to acquire virtue and scientific truth."[4]

And yet, important though medicine might be, it was not, in Maimonides' view, equivalent to achieving a knowledge of God per se. In the *Mishneh Torah* he stated unequivocally: "Man must direct his heart and every one of his actions solely toward knowing God."[5] Also: "When a man reflects on these things, studies all these created beings, from the angels and spheres down to human beings and so on, and realizes the divine wisdom manifested in them all, his love for God will increase, his soul will thirst, his very flesh will yearn, to love God."[6] However important medical knowledge might be as knowledge for its own sake, its true value lay in serving a higher claim.

Science was then, for Maimonides, a means to an end, the study of the works of God that might ultimately lead to him, just as the study of the works of an author might lead to the knowledge of that author him- or herself. Maybe for that reason, Maimonides, following Avicenna, dwelt on the theoretical aspect of medicine, and was wary of proceeding when he was not totally confident of the full medical literature that would explain the declared symptoms. According to the twelfth-century historian Ali ibn Yusuf al-Qifti (though his account has been questioned by some scholars),[7] Maimonides showed himself at times reluctant to apply whatever theoretical medical knowledge he had acquired, whether due to professional caution or not, we cannot know. He would have recalled the Talmudic warning that "the best of doctors are destined for hell" and the cautionary comment on this passage by Rashi: "The best doctors go to hell. They do not fear sickness. They eat the food of the healthy, and they do not act humbly before God. Sometimes they kill, and sometimes they are able to heal a poor person but do not do so."[8]

Maimonides treated diseases by following the scientific method—that is to say, not by guesswork, as many of his contemporaries did, or by rule of thumb, as proposed in certain popular medical handbooks, but by making decisions based on documentary evidence. This strictly disciplined attitude stemmed from his religious belief that the preservation of life was a divine commandment, and that therefore a physician had to enter fully armed with the necessary knowledge. "When you think of cutting out something of the body, keep in mind three intentions," he wrote. "The first, that your work shall be finished in the shortest time possible; the second, that no pain at all shall be caused; the third, that you be sure of the result. However, the result will require three intentions. First, be clearly aware that your intentions will be attained with certainty; second, if this cannot be achieved, at least that no damage shall ensue from side effects; third, be sure that the disease shall not relapse. Then, when you consider these intentions, it will be evident to you that at times surgical and at times medicinal treatment will be the more praiseworthy."[9] Medical doctors today would agree with Maimonides.

In a letter written in 1196 to his translator, the Provençal scholar Samuel ibn Tibbon, Maimonides outlined his increased daily labors as the court physician:

> My duties to the Sultan are very heavy. I am obliged to visit him every day, early in the morning, and when he or any of his children or concubines are indisposed, I cannot leave Cairo but must stay during most of the day in the palace. It also frequently happens that one or two of the officers fall sick and I must attend to their healing. Hence, as a rule, every day, early in the morning, I go to Cairo and, even if nothing unusual happens there, I do not return to Fustat until the afternoon. Then I am famished but I find the antechambers filled with people, both Jews and Gentiles, nobles and common people, judges and policemen, friends and enemies—a mixed multitude who await the time of my return. I dismount from my animal, wash my hands, go forth to my patients, and entreat them to bear with me while I partake of some light refreshment, the only meal I eat in twenty-four hours. Then I go to attend to my patients and write prescriptions and directions for their ailments. Patients go in and out until nightfall, and sometimes, even as the Torah is my faith, until two hours and more into the night. I converse with them and prescribe for them even while lying down from sheer fatigue. When night falls, I am so exhausted that I can hardly speak.[10]

Another letter, this one addressed to the new sultan 'Umar ibn Nur al-Din, cautiously recommends the salutary drinking of wine (Maimonides dared recommend to a Muslim patient, and a sultan no less, this alcoholic treatment at the time for depression), and proceeds to outline clearly his medical credo. Maimonides begins by confessing that his poor constitution and the weakness of his natural faculties—present already in his youth, and even more apparent in his old age—constitute a barrier between him and many pleasures: "I do not mean pleasures, rather good deeds, the most important and elevated of which is to serve our Master in actual practice." He continues: "Our Master should not criticize his humble servant for having mentioned the use of wine and songs, both of which are abhorred by the religion. For this servant did not command acting in this manner; he merely stated that which is dictated by his profession. Indeed, the religious legislators know, as do the physicians, that wine has benefits for man"—not for the sake of sensual gratification, such as appears, for instance, in the works of the ninth-century Hebrew poet Dunash ben Labrat, "Drink, he said, don't drowse, / Drink wine aged well in barrels, / near henna beds and aloes / and roses mixed with myrrh"—but in a strictly medicinal sense. "A physician is bound, inasmuch as he is a physician, to present with a beneficial regimen, whether it is forbidden or permitted; the patient is endowed with the freedom to choose whether to follow or not. If he fails to mention everything that may be helpful, be it forbidden or permitted, he is guilty of acting dishonestly, for he did not offer trustworthy advice."[11]

Maimonides now distinguishes between medical instructions and religious commandments.

> It is well known that religious law commands what is beneficial and prohibits what is harmful with respect to the world-to-come. The physician, on the other hand, instructs what will benefit the body and warns about what will harm it in this world. The difference between religious commandments and medical counsel is that religion commands and coerces a

person to do what will benefit him in the future, and prohibits what will harm him in the future, and punishes for it. The physician, on the other hand, counsels [his patient] about what will benefit him, and warns him about what will cause him harm. He does not use coercion, nor does he punish; he merely presents the information to the patient in the manner of advice. And it is [the patient's] choice [whether to follow that advice].

Maimonides concludes:

The reason for this is obvious. The harm and benefit from a medical perspective are immediate and clearly evident. Thus, there is no need for coercion or punishment. As for religious commandments, however, the harm and benefit that they bring are not evident in this world. The fool might, therefore, imagine to himself that everything that is said to be harmful is not harmful, and everything that is said to be beneficial is not beneficial because these things are not clearly evident to him. For this reason religious law compels one to practice good and punishes for doing evil, for the good and evil will only become apparent in the world to come. All this is benevolence toward us, a favor to us in light of our foolishness, mercy upon us owing to the weakness of our understanding.

Maimonides' medical knowledge was extensive and his physician's eye as sharp as when, as a legal scholar, he scrutinized the tenets of Jewish and Islamic law. Commenting on the works of Galen and Hippocrates, Maimonides brought to these classical texts his rational point of view. Where Hippocrates notes that "A boy is born from the right ovary, a girl from the left," Maimonides ironically observes, "A man would have to be either prophet or genius to know this."[12] In his own book of medical aphorisms written in Arabic, the *Fusul Musa*, Maimonides collected observations handed down by notable Greco-Persian medical writers for the use of medical practitioners. The book

The three great ancient teachers of medicine: Galen (Roman),
Avicenna (Persian), and Hippocrates (Greek), fifteenth century, woodcut.
(Photo: Everett Collection Historical/Alamy Stock Photo)

consists of twenty-five sections, each dealing with a different
area of medicine: anatomy, physiology, pathology, symptom-
atology and diagnosis, etiology of disease and therapeutics, fevers, bloodletting, laxatives and emetics, surgery, gynecology,
hygiene, bathing, diet, drugs, and medical curiosities. Maimonides' curiosity was all-embracing.

Astrology interested him as well, but merely to refute it as a
superstitious practice: in this field he remained a stern skeptic.
In a letter to Jewish scholars from southern France written in
1194, Maimonides gave his opinion on the claims of astrologers
(which he considered dangerous charlatanism) and laid out the
conditions for accepting a proposition as a scientific fact:

> It is not proper for a man to accept as trustworthy anything
> other than one of these three things. The first is a thing for

which there is a clear proof deriving from man's reasoning—such as arithmetic, geometry, and astronomy. The second is a thing that a man perceives through one of the five senses—such as when he knows with certainty that this is red and this is black and the like through the sight of his eye; or as when he tastes that this is bitter and this is sweet; or as when he feels that this is hot and this is cold; or as when he hears that this sound is clear and this sound is indistinct; or as when he smells that this is a pleasing smell and this is a displeasing smell and the like. The third is a thing that a man receives from the prophets or from the righteous. Every reasonable man ought to distinguish in his mind and thought all the things that he accepts as trustworthy, and say: "This I accept as trustworthy because of tradition, and this because of sense-perception, and this on grounds of reason." Anyone who accepts as trustworthy anything that is not of these three species, of him it is said: "The simple believes everything" (Prov. 14:15). Thus you ought to know that fools have composed thousands of books of nothingness and emptiness. Any number of men, great in years but not in wisdom, wasted all their days in studying these books and imagined that these follies are science.[13]

In his ten medical works, all written in Arabic, Maimonides attempted to systematize unwieldy and scattered medical information from classical sources together with observations culled from his own experience, exploring every aspect of the ailment he was treating in the patient, and also in the patient's natural environment. "It is well known among the physicians," writes Maimonides in the preface to his *Treatise on Asthma*, "that this disease can have many causes and that the regulation of the healing of diseases differs according to the different causes. And it is well known among the physicians that one cannot treat a disease in a proper way unless one has first examined the temperament of the patient in general and the temperament of every organ in particular. . . . And then one should examine his age, the condition of his town, his habit, the time of year, and the temperament of the weather at the moment."[14]

Maimonides wrote the *Treatise on Asthma* for a patient who consulted him about his violent headaches, which prevented him from wearing a turban. The patient, whom Maimonides diagnosed as suffering from chronic asthma, asked whether a change of climate might be good for him. His symptoms, the patient said, had begun with a common cold that made his lungs feel congested, especially in the rainy season, forcing him to gasp for air. Maimonides laid out for the patient's benefit dietary rules specifically suited for asthmatics, proposing recipes for proper food and drugs, and suggesting that travel to several zones of the Middle East might relieve his suffering.

Likewise, in his *Treatise on Hemorrhoids*, Maimonides lists therapeutic measures to alleviate the ailment, such as sitz baths, oils and fumigations, and certain foods that might ease the patient's pain. In the case of this ailment, Maimonides disapproves of surgery because (he notes with perspicacity) surgery does not remove the underlying causes that produced the hemorrhoids in the first place. Maimonides was a holistic healer.

As with these two treatises, many of Maimonides' medical works were the result of a consultation, whether on the health of the body or a disturbance of the spirit. Sometimes the ailment concerned both, as was the case of the new ruler, Saladin's successor, the aforementioned Nur Al-Din. Nur Al-Din was a man with a scholarly taste for religious problems, particularly those related to the school of Sufism, noted for his piety and personal bravery, and also for his worldly passion for sex. Of him it could be said what Edward Gibbon said about another sovereign of similar tastes, the Roman Emperor Gordian: "Twenty-two acknowledged concubines and a library of sixty-two thousand volumes attested the variety of his inclinations; and from the productions which he left behind him, it appears that the former as well as the latter were designed for use rather than for ostentation."[15] Nur Al-Din, keen to augment his sexual potency, consulted Maimonides. Maimonides advised judicious moderation. Both in the *Treatise on Cohabitation* which he wrote for Nur Al-Din, consisting of a number of gastronomical and pharmaceutical recipes which can either arouse or diminish sexual activity, and in the *Treatise on Asthma*, he explained, "As for [unrestrained] sexual intercourse, it is well known—even to the masses—that it is very harmful to most people and that excessive indulgence in it is harmful to all people. . . . A man should therefore decrease his accustomed sexual activity as he becomes more advanced in years."[16] We do not know if Nur Al-Din followed Maimonides' advice.

6

Maimonides the Scholar

Naked without cover or dress
utterly soulless, and hollow—
from its mouth come wisdom and prudence
and in ambush it kills like an arrow

> —Solomon ibn Gabirol, "The Pen"
> (eleventh century)

THE QUESTION of why Maimonides, like most other Jewish intellectuals of al-Andalus, chose to write most of his texts in Arabic or Judeo-Arabic (a continuum of Jewish varieties of the Arabic tongue written in Hebrew letters) has not been satisfactorily answered. Some scholars suggest that there might have been no conscious motive for this decision. "In view of the extensive adjustment of the Jews under Islam, and the degree to which they identified themselves with its culture, nothing is more natural than that they should use in their writings the language which served them in every other need. It simply did not occur to them in their prose works to choose Hebrew as a mark of identification."[1] In any case, Judeo-Arabic was the language of choice of the Jews of al-Andalus.

Maimonides himself wrote in Hebrew as well as Arabic and Judeo-Arabic. Works written in languages other than Arabic and Hebrew were available to him and his fellow scholars in translation, a highly developed art in the Arab world, particularly Córdoba and Baghdad. Writing in 1199 to his own translator, Samuel ibn Tibbon, Maimonides recommended a method that chose style over literality. "The translator who proposes to render each word literally and adhere slavishly to the order of the words and sentences in the original," he warned, "will meet much difficulty, and the result will be doubtful and corrupt. This is not the right method. The translator should first try to grasp the sense of the subject thoroughly, and then state the theme with perfect clarity in the other language. This, however, cannot be done without changing the order of the words, putting many words for one word, or *vice versa*, and adding or taking away words, so that the subject be perfectly intelligible in the language into which he translates."[2] Unfortunately, Ibn Tibbon did not follow Maimonides' advice, and his 1204 translation of *The Guide of the Perplexed* into Hebrew was criticized for sticking too closely to the original, using Arab neologisms and borrowing from Arabic philosophical vocabulary. Ibn Tibbon's excuse, however, would have been that many of the words used by Maimonides in his Arabic writings were unavailable in Hebrew.[3]

Maimonides would have learned from his erudite father and his Córdoba circle the importance of studying not only the essential books of the Jewish faith but also works from the Islamic culture and from the ancient Greek. Education of a Jewish child was rooted in the admonition God gives David which he passes on to his son Solomon: "Know the God of your father, and serve Him with single mind and fervent heart" (1 Chronicles 28:9). This commandment seeks to secure the ties between father and son through the worship of the same God, to know and serve him to the best of one's abilities, not only with the heart but with the mind as well. Implied in this essential commandment are the obligations of teaching and of learning, of passing on and receiving acquired knowledge as well as the instruments for reaching farther, studying the unchanging and unchangeable text from one generation to the next.

However, Maimon the father and Moses the son differed in their approach to the study of the Word. The father was an enthusiastic believer, as much in love with the profound teachings of the Torah as with the stories of the Talmud, trusting his imagination to deal with the faces of angels and with the God who walked in the Garden in the cool of the evening. The son sought in the holy books logical answers to rational questions, and believed utterly in the power of philosophy to glean the divine truth bereft of the adornments of imagistic fantasy. Scholarly inquiry and unquestioning faith were not seen as opposites by the student Maimonides, and he required no fantastical tales to secure his attention.

It is possible to see a notable feature of Maimonides' personality in this strict adherence to legal and factual language, and in the invention of the precise terms he needed when he could not find them in the traditional writings. Maimonides' eye falls on the information that the text provides, whether sacred or medical, and in analyzing it he displays astonishing ingenuity in his exegetic imagination and in his use of rhetorical strategies.[4] Style, of course, is important to him because it does the author's (or Author's) best to convey the intended meaning and educate its intended audience. Even the choice of language is important because, as Maimonides understood, after Babel, a person is identified by the tongue he speaks and is molded by that tongue. Though nowhere in his writings does Maimonides explicitly lay out a systematic theory of language, it is evident that he recognizes the importance of linguistics. Maimonides appears interested from a practical point of view in how the human mind receives and expresses itself differently according to the language it employs, and according to the intention of the discourse, its instructive strategies and its selected subject, whether in the description of a physical ailment, the intricate problems of prophecy, or the subtleties of a Talmudic argument. As a reader of the tenth-century Islamic philosopher Abu Nasr Al-Farabi (whom he overwhelmingly praises) and Avicenna, both of whom developed in their writings linguistic theories, Maimonides was aware of the importance of learning and putting to good use the rhetorician's art. Al-Farabi maintained that one of the prime obligations of a philosopher is to translate the erroneous or misleading idioms of common speech into a logically ordered grammar of thought. Maimonides takes this requirement one step farther, and demonstrates, in the act of composing his books, that this "translation" can be applied to all subjects, including holy ones, except (as he stresses in the *Guide*) to the recognition of the truth of God, even in interiorized thought. At this frontier, language ceases to be effective and "power fails the lofty fantasy."[5] This recognition of linguistic want is not in contradiction to the rationalistic mind: on the contrary, it affirms it with awareness and humility. Everything that can be put into words lies within the scope of reason. But then again, not everything can be put into words.

Many years later, as an older man celebrated for his wisdom, Maimonides would refute the notion of intellectual authority being hereditary. The art of translation in all its manifestations is the art of self-definition: literal translation from one tongue to another; translation understood as metaphor, as the carrying of one verbal construct from one verbal realm to a different one; the conversion of an intellectual inheritance into a personal one, both from one's elders and from scholars from the past. Out of the experience bequeathed in the words of others the recipient refashions and subsumes whatever his or her intellect deems important or inspiring. There is no dogmatic obligation in matters of intellectual education, and no arranged marriage of minds produces healthy offspring. Only sufficient intelligence is required; poor judgment will lead to making the wrong choice.

This chosen scholarly inheritance overrides that of one's own flesh and blood. A Talmudic saying instructs: "Fit thyself for the study of the law (Torah), for the [knowledge of] it is not thine inheritance."[6] Maimonides, while expressing in his last years a "highly positive evaluation" of his son Avraham, did not involve Avraham in his own official activities in Egypt, nor did he decree that Avraham or his descendants succeed him in his high office as head of the Jewish community of Fustat, perhaps because he wished that his son forge his path himself, which (as we have said) Avraham successfully did.[7] This is the course Maimonides had chosen as a scholar possessed with erudition and philological skills: when he refers to his "elders" in his writings, he means his intellectual masters, such as Isaac Alfasi, author of one of the first essential studies of halakhic literature, and his father's own teacher, the Talmudic scholar Joseph Halevi ibn Migash, both of whom died before Maimonides was born. In this attitude toward inherited experience, Maimonides rejoins the Roman Seneca in his advice to a would-be philosopher: Socrates, Cleanthes, Plato, Seneca pronounced, "they are all your ancestors, if you conduct yourself in a manner worthy of them."[8] And as a medical doctor, a halakhic scholar, and a philosopher, Maimonides sought in a host of gifted ancestors answers to age-old questions and instruction for his day.

7

Maimonides the Philosopher

> This man then, answered Aristotle, was by birth a
> Jew. . . . This race has its origin in the philosophers
> who live among the Indians.
>
> —Clearchus of Soli (third century BCE)

THE ORAL LAW was known as "the tradition received from
the fathers." It is likely that these fathers, in what is known as
the "classical" or Tannaitic era of rabbinical law from the first
century BCE, borrowed ideas from their Greek counterparts,
perhaps through the influence of the learned Jews of Alexandria. There are essential concepts and methods of argumentation appearing in the Greek classical texts that were echoed or
adapted in those of Jewish thought, and the rabbinic methods
of interpretation that produced the opinions and precepts later
collected in the Talmud derived perhaps in part from the theories of Hellenistic rhetoric.[1]

This interweaving of Greek and Jewish thought has legendary origins. According to the Jewish-Roman historian Fla-

vius Josephus, of the first century CE, a disciple of Aristotle, one Clearchus of Soli, reported that his master had met a Jew well versed in philosophy who had settled among the Greeks and "communicated to us more information than that which he received from us."[2] Clearchus was a scholar of Eastern civilizations, keen on finding bridges between different cultures; he suggested that the Jewish people might be descendants of the gymnosophists, a sect of contemplative ascetics of India, heirs of the ancient Persian magi. In the city of Bactria near the frontier with India, Clearchus left an inscription, copied from the sanctuary of Delphi, outlining his recommended code of behavior:

> As children, learn good manners.
> As young men, learn to control the passions.
> In middle age, be just.
> In old age, give good advice.
> Then die, without regret.[3]

Josephus's story has its counterpart in Islamic culture. The tale starts in a dream one night in the ninth century in Baghdad. Caliph al-Ma'mun, known as "Lover of Knowledge" and son of the famous Harun al-Rashid (who, as a character in the *Arabian Nights*, would delight the Western imagination in later centuries), saw in his sleep a pale, blue-eyed man with a broad forehead and frowning eyebrows. With the assurance of dreamers, the caliph understood that the stranger was Aristotle. Al-Ma'mun and Aristotle conversed all night long. In the morning, as a result of the encounter, the caliph ordered that a library be founded that would house a translation center devoted mainly to the works of the philosopher. The center was placed under the direction of the Christian medical scholar Hunayn ibn Ishaq, who, assisted by a school of disciples, translated into Syriac and Arabic almost the entire corpus of Greek and Hellenistic philosophy and science known at the time.[4] A contemporary of

Hunayn, Al-Kindi, became the first *faylasuf*, or interpreter of Islamic doctrine through rationalist thought, attempting to blend the Aristotelian, Peripatetic, and Neoplatonist doctrines with Islamic dogma. Among the texts translated from the Greek by al-Ma'mun's scholars were Aristotle's *Metaphysics* and *On the Heavens*, a few of the cosmological writings of Alexander of Aphrodisias, three books of Plotinus's *Enneads*, and Proclus's *Elements of Theology*, all fundamental readings for Maimonides. Later the discovery of other writings by Aristotle (some two hundred treatises, of which only thirty-one have survived) provided work for the next generation of translators and elicited a different, more comprehensive approach from its readers. Al-Farabi, for example, whom Maimonides studied in depth, based his pedagogical project on the totality of Aristotle's writings then available, considering them not as piecemeal treatises but as chapters of a systematic whole ruled by dialectic demonstration. On the basis of Aristotle's work, together with translations of Euclid, Ptolemy, Hippocrates, and Galen, Al-Farabi composed a college curriculum that interwove Greek philosophy, Islamic science, and the study of the liberal arts. Avicenna as well argued for a study chart that incorporated cross-cultural texts on logic, philosophy, and theology, and proposed a rich academic program that would assist the incipient soul to engage in "a spiritual, secret conversation" with the All-Knowing, fount of all wisdom.[5] Two centuries later, Maimonides' contemporary Averroës, attempting to expose the demonstrative sciences as an organized single entity, resorted as well to all these Greek sources—to Aristotle above all.[6]

Aristotle believed that there was an essential difference between what we can know and our understanding of the reasons behind that knowledge within our grasp, distinguishing the questions arising from theoretical science from more practically oriented demands. In his *On the Soul*, Aristotle had written that "knowing something about things differing from one another

Aristotle, woodcut by T. Stimmer [?], 1589. (© Wellcome Collection)

is considered honourable either in virtue of exactness or because those are known through things more splendid and more noble." Averroës, in his commentary on this passage, explained: "By *exactness* he means the confirmation associated with demonstration. By what he said: *or because they are known through things more noble*, he means the nobility of the subject."[7] Logic, Aristotle believed, and Averroës explained, can point toward what one should think, the "noble" subjects, and can help us set out a method for developing the connected concepts of truth, predication, and definition. This reasonable approach to fundamental questions proved very attractive to Jewish thinkers. Philo of Alexandria argued that God did not thrust human beings into the world to fumble aimlessly in search of such answers. Philo, like Aristotle before him and Maimonides after, believed that factual evidence filtered through human reason must light the way to the truth, and that we should not put our trust in the superstitious fictions of divination and astrology. Aristotle argued that we hold, up to a certain point, control of our fate, and that fate is not entirely reliant on a predetermined system based on necessity. Rejecting the notion of an obligatory passage from what is given as true to what is arguably necessary, Aristotle concludes that not everything that happens happens out of need. "What is, necessarily is, when it is," he pronounced gnomically, "and what is not, necessarily is not, when it is not."[8] Only the laws of nature are consequential: as smoke must ascend and autumn leaves must fall, humans must die, but no alignment of the stars can tell us when or how. Philo agreed. "How long shall we, the aged," Philo asks with bitter humor, "be children grown old in our bodies through length of time, but just infants in our souls out of a lack of sense, considering the most incalculable element, fortune, to be the most persistent, but nature, the firmest element, to be the most unsteady? We change and switch our actions, as if engaged in board games, thinking that fortune's gifts are more stable than nature's, and nature's more insecure than fortune's."[9]

For centuries, religious thinkers were reluctant to allow philosophical questions to enter the realm of theology. The study of religion was seen as frankly opposed to that of philosophy, and the defense of philosophy was equated to the annihilation of religion because (the detractors assumed) it allowed doubt to enter the realm of faith. Perhaps the first known expression of this reluctance can be found in Demosthenes, who in the fourth century BCE observed, "What each man wishes, that he also believes to be true."[10] Faith is not to be either reasoned or questioned.

The historian Hermann Cohen, in 1915, argued that the basic difference between Christian and Jewish theology lies in the fact that for the former, philosophy and religion are separate fields, while for the latter, at least for Maimonides and his followers, this opposition is invalid.[11] Considering philosophy to be an integral part of Jewish faith, Maimonides redeemed the value of philosophical doubt and ontological inquiry. His task, as he saw it, was to make people aware of the Law of God, not only to accept it as a commandment but to understand its contents. And in order to do this, he required the craft of logical thinking as well as the art of rhetoric. To spend a life dedicated to the question of God seemed to him in perfect accordance with Aristotle's principle of a life dedicated to the intellect. For Aristotle, as earlier for Socrates, this meant that the practice of reason would lead to the knowledge of self. "If then the intellect is something divine in comparison with man," Aristotle wrote, "so is the life of the intellect divine in comparison with human life."[12] "The only difference," notes the French philosopher Pierre Bouretz in his study of Maimonides' philosophy, "is that in the case of the latter, it becomes synonymous with the knowledge of God."[13]

Socrates had taught his philosophy through what he called maieutics, or midwifery, helping to give birth to his questioners' latent ideas by questioning them in turn. Maimonides' method was a different one: to try to provide answers, or at least to apply an investigative methodology to the disturbing perplexities in the questioner's mind. Maimonides' method when offering advice followed the tempered style of the great Talmudic commentators who endeavored to look at as many aspects of the problem as possible, from several varying points of view, turning a question in all conceivable ways, not necessarily to come to a definitive solution but to enrich the original thought in a process of ongoing interrogation and exchange.

Often Maimonides seems to take up both sides of a Talmudic *be-mai-peligei* strategy (literally, "On what do they disagree?") that serves to illustrate, in the first place, how the area of disagreement is made visible by inference and, in the second, how seemingly contradictory points of view might be opposed in some things but in accord in others. One classic example of this appears in the Babylonian Talmud, tractate Temurah, where the rabbinic commentators Rava and Abaye discuss the question of whether a transaction which breaches a religious law can have legal validity. Rava's opinion is that in general terms it does not, Abaye sustains the contrary; however, they agree on a number of particular examples of the problem, though they differ on which is the general rule and which the exception.

Maimonides was once consulted about a case in which a scholar had interrupted a sermon by the head of the congregation and accused the lecturer of speaking nonsense. The question put to Maimonides was, Should the scholar be punished? Maimonides answered as a mai-peligei philosopher: since the sermon contained nothing "worthy of reproach," the critic had "very grievously transgressed by humiliating another person in public without cause." However, since the scholar was "known for his piety and wisdom, it [was] improper to speak about him until he himself [was] heard, for the sacred Torah requires us to honor scholars and give them the benefit of the doubt."[14] In other words, the congregation could have its dialectical cake and eat it too.

Maimonides believed that there was no contradiction between the truths revealed by God and those perceived through rational inference by an honest and enlightened mind, and he wished to suppress the age-old doubts between debates about the Law and the arguments of philosophical inquiry, a conflicted state that he encapsulated in the notion of *nevukhim*, "perplexity."[15] In Exodus, the translators of the King James Bible have the Pharaoh say of the Israelites that they were "entangled in the land" ("astray," "confused," "confounded," "wandering aimlessly," as other translations have it; Exodus 14:3). The Maimonides scholar Leo Strauss has argued that this perplexity is not epistemological but political, and that any questions about the basis of knowledge that can be asked must necessarily be preceded by the question of what it means to philosophize within the framework of the authority of the Law. According to Strauss, Maimonides can resort to philosophy to explain the meaning of the Law, but philosophy cannot lead to the Law itself. The Law, says Strauss, is the pre-philosophical context of philosophy as well as its framework.[16]

Maimonides was aware of this: he thought of the Law in terms not only of philosophical reflection but especially of legal practice. This dialogue between legal theory and its practice is everywhere evident in Aristotle, as it is in Plato and most of the Greek philosophers.[17] It is important to note that while exploring, as a learned scholar, the theories and canonical precepts of Jewish identity, rendered legitimate by a highly systematized type of normative rabbinic Judaism, Maimonides admitted (sometimes even encouraged) Jewish practices outside orthodox public worship and the dictates of rabbinical courts, practices that departed significantly from the traditional norms.[18] For

Maimonides, scholarly halakhic investigations and the conventional everyday practice of the Law were meant to coexist.

Convinced of the usefulness of the ancient Greek sources as an instrument for clarifying the problems of Jewish thought, Maimonides persisted in his quest. To his disciple and translator Samuel ibn Tibbon, Maimonides emphatically recommended the study of Aristotle: "For Aristotle reached the highest level of knowledge to which man can ascend, with the exception of one who experiences the emanation of the Divine Spirit." And he added, in deference to Aristotle's Arab translators, "Be careful not to study the works of Aristotle without help of his commentators such as Alexander [of Aphrodisias, in the third century] Themistus [sixth-century deacon of Alexandria] or Averroes."[19] Maimonides knew that translators can be the best and keenest of readers.

In recommending the study of Aristotle, Maimonides makes clear his belief that we "should accept the truth from whatever source it proceeds."[20] He understood that, drawing from the various sources of human knowledge and experience, the inconstant nature of the world could come to be understood rationally. This, of course, within individual limits, but limits that were not necessarily obstacles to reach the truth but further starting points for fruitful inquiry. His magnificent aspiration was to transform Judaism into "a religion of reason."[21] Yet reason was one of the only two ways to reach God's truth; the other was illuminated faith, which transcends the frontiers of thought and grants us occasional epiphanies. The first is comparable to Plato's *episteme* (knowledge); the second to *doxa* (belief), which, Aristotle argued, was the starting point on the path to knowledge.[22] Samuel Taylor Coleridge in 1830 remarked that "every man is born an Aristotelian or a Platonist."[23] Perhaps Maimonides, believing in the reality of ideas and also in the need to approach ideas empirically, can be said to have been both.

Seneca, following the tenets of Aristotelian thought, had

argued that reason has a divine origin, and that to follow the dictates of reason brings us closer to the truth. "God is near you, he is with you, he is within you," Seneca admonishes. "A holy spirit indwells within us, one who marks our good and bad deeds, and is our guardian. As we treat this spirit, so are we treated by it. Indeed, no man can be good without the help of God. Can one rise superior to fortune unless God helps him to rise? He it is that gives noble and upright counsel."[24] The goal of Stoic thinkers such as Seneca was always to be guided by that holy spirit. Maimonides, while not commonly associated with Stoic philosophy, put it in terms of illuminating *giluy Shekhinah*, "a revealing of the *Shekhinah*, the innate presence of God in the world." "We are," Maimonides wrote, "like someone in a very dark night over whom lightning flashes time and time again."[25]

The ties between Maimonides' philosophical inquiries and those of Aristotle have long been the subject of controversy. Certain rabbinical commentators argue that, for instance, the doctrine of the mean (according to which virtue is the intermediate state between two extremes), while existing in Aristotle and reduced to the popular saying "Nothing in excess," becomes "a totally new and uniquely Jewish creation" after being "converted" in the teachings of Maimonides.[26] Centuries later, Immanuel Kant derided the Aristotelian concept of the mean: "To be much too virtuous, i.e. to adhere too closely to one's duty, would be like making a circle much too round or a straight line much too straight."[27] Maimonides thought otherwise.

Maimonides understood that Aristotle's concept of the mean was not limited to moral virtue achieved through a contemplative life but covered every field in the natural world, as well as that of creation. Maimonides does not offer a discussion of the mean's origins but simply states that it is an established truth and does not require further evidence to support it. The universe, says Maimonides, was created according to the mean, and for this reason it cannot change. Something can only change because of an excess in it that can be removed or a deficiency that can be added in order to make it better. However, following the universal mean, since the work of God is by definition perfect, it is not susceptible to alteration. The reader can sense in these words the urge to affirm the eternal constancy of the Lord while at the same time remaining aware of the constant changes of a life in exile.

Maimonides wanted his brethren to come of age under the certainty that God, trusting his creation, had given them an infallible chart by which to steer themselves in the light of their intellect. God delivered the Torah to Moses on Mount Sinai, and because he does not want us to lose our way in the darkness of ignorance (the Talmudists added), he permitted or commanded the study of the Torah's mysteries to allow us to approach with some degree of understanding the bewildering ways of the universe that only God understands in full.

The Talmudists believed that the Torah contained everything: in the books that Moses received on Mount Sinai, every question, and the answer to every question, was to be found. A Talmudic story exemplifies this belief:

> When Moses ascended on high [to receive the Torah] he found the Holy One, blessed be He, engaged in affixing *tagin* [crownlike flourishes] to the letters. Moses said: "Lord of the Universe, who stays Thy hand?" [that is, is there anything lacking in the Torah so that these ornaments are necessary?] He replied: "There will arise a man at the end of many generations, Akiba ben Yosef by name, who will expound, upon each tiny speck, heaps and heaps of laws." "Lord of the Universe," said Moses, "permit me to see him." He replied: "Turn thee round." Moses went [into the academy of Rabbi Akiba] and sat down behind eight rows [of Akiba's disciples]. Not being able to follow their arguments he was ill at ease, but when they came to a certain subject and the disciples said to

the master "Whence do you know it?" and the latter replied, "It is a law given to Moses at Sinai," he was comforted.[28]

The Torah, the Hebrew Bible, and the Old Testament are three different books whose usages vary and sometimes overlap. In rabbinical literature, the Torah is understood to be the Pentateuch, consisting of the five books of Moses—Genesis, Exodus, Leviticus, Numbers, and Deuteronomy—but it can also encompass all written and oral Jewish tradition. The Hebrew Bible, also known as Tanakh, comprises the twenty-four books from Genesis to Chronicles, set down in its final form around 450 BCE, and can also mean the Hebrew Bible with its exegetic commentaries on the same page as the main text. The order of the Tanakh is not that of the Old Testament in modern Christian Bibles. The theologian Jack Miles notes that in the Tanakh the narration proceeds "from action to speech to silence"—first Genesis and Exodus, then the prophetic books, and finally what Miles calls "the books of silence," Job, Lamentations, Ecclesiastes, and Esther—while in the Old Testament it goes "from action to silence to speech," since in the latter the prophetic books are moved from the middle to the end.[29] Readers know that the order in which the chapters of a book are read, whether a modern novel or the Bible, defines the book. Like the rabbis of old, Maimonides the philosopher understood that silence must come after speech.

Human understanding, as the People of the Book learned of old, comes through the use of the word: in reading, thought, dialogue, debate, and the personal reflection that follows or precedes action. For the Jewish people, this personal relationship of a reader with his or her books has always been a primordial duty. The daily study of the Torah is an obligation so essential that, according to Judah the Prince, "During the first three [hours of the day], the Holy One, Blessed be He, sits and engages in Torah study."[30] And if the longed-for flashes of understanding are ever to be granted, this task must be undertaken through reason. That is why, among most Jews, the occupation of a scholar is esteemed above all others.

This need for "spiritual, secret conversation" with the Word of God was held true by the early Christians. After the Reformation, however, the Catholic Church deemed it advisable for believers, with the exception of scholarly theologians, to approach the biblical text only through the intermediary of their priest. In opposition to this, the Protestant reformer William Tyndale argued that "each man should help himself to the sacred bread by which he may satisfy his hungry soul."[31] In 1536, as a reward for his encouragements, Tyndale was charged with heresy and executed by strangulation, and his body was burned.

Not every personal engagement with the Word of God met Maimonides' unconditional approval. In the final sections of the first part of *The Guide of the Perplexed*, Maimonides argues against the Mutakallim, followers of an Islamic school of rational theology called Ilm-al-Kalam, who sought in philosophical demonstrations confirmation of their religious principles and whose ideas had taken root in Jewish philosophical circles. The Jewish Mutakallim developed as a reaction to the Islamic school. The earliest known work by a Jewish philosopher of the Mutakallim school is the tenth-century *Emunot ve-De'ot*, or *Book of Beliefs and Opinions*, by Saadia Gaon, otherwise famous for his *Prayer Book* (thought to be the first effort to systematize the Jewish prayer service) as well as for his work on Hebrew linguistics and Jewish law. In the *Opinions*, Saadia Gaon discusses the problems set out earlier by the Mutakallim: the question of creation, the unity of God, the divine attributes, and the nature of the soul. For Saadia Gaon, God created the world ex nihilo, as is proclaimed in the Torah. To prove the unity of God, he used the demonstrations of the Mutakallim, according to whom only the attributes of essence can be ascribed to God, not the attributes of action. For the soul, however, Saadia Gaon argued, the matter is otherwise: "If the soul be an accident only, it can itself have no such accidents as wisdom, joy, love."[32] And the soul, he explained, possessed all of these.

Addressing himself directly to the Islamic source, Maimonides argued that most of these propositions are untenable, and he regarded them as founded not on positive facts but on imaginative fiction. The Mutakallim, according to Maimonides, denied the existence of any law that might stand for an organizing principle or unity in the universe. For the Mutakallim, the various parts of the universe are independent one from another; they consist of equal elements and are not composed of substance and properties, but of atoms and accidents. In their view, the law of causality is invalid and human actions are not the result of will and design but of mere fortuitous accidents. All this, Maimonides recognized, was contrary to the Aristotelian principle of the universe as one organized body, every part of which has an active and individual relation to it, as Maimonides also believed. Maimonides' criticism is especially directed toward the Mutakallim's maxim according to which everything that is conceivable by the imagination is admissible. This smacked of fairy tales and impossible fantasies, and the idea was profoundly repugnant to Maimonides' rational mind.

"The study of Truth," Aristotle had declared, "is in one sense difficult, in another easy. This is shown by the fact that whereas no one person can obtain an adequate grasp of it, we cannot *all* fail in the attempt . . . just as it is with bats' eyes in respect of daylight, so it is with our mental intelligence in respect of those things which are by nature most obvious."[33] This is the paradox: our universe is essentially mysterious and will remain so, but human reason persists in searching for its truth because (Aristotle again) the very existence of that truth, however inscrutable, constrains us to search for it, demanding that we unveil it but hiding its face in the process. In this paradoxical quest, as Philo of Alexandria pointed out, "whenever the mind begins to know itself and to engage with mental objects, it will thrust away that part of the soul which inclines toward the sense-perceptible image"[34] and hope to reach an understanding of that which lies beyond the realm of words.

Maimonides admitted that questions about the reason for certain particular aspects of the world can indeed be validly pursued in a scholarly quest. The prophet Isaiah had asked, "Do you not know? Have you not heard? Have you not been told from the very first? Have you not discerned How the earth was founded?" (Isaiah 40:21). These questions are therefore valid pursuits. But to seek God's intention in creating the universe as a whole, and not just "from the foundations of the earth," is a meaningless and forbidden inquiry. While a philosopher can consider the purpose of any given event or object in its relationship to other events and other objects—a person, a dog, a tree (because, since they exist, they must have certain attributes about which one can inquire the purpose, such as capacity for thought, sense of smell, a tendency to grow toward the light)—the question of why the universe exists is beyond the scope and capabilities of the philosopher's mind. "One must not . . . seek the final end of what has not been produced in time," Maimonides writes in the *Guide*.[35]

This, however, is an essential problem that stems from the very concept of divine creation: was creation the result of a cause-and-effect relation, or purely the demonstration of the free activity of divine will? Was Plato right in suggesting that the world exists in eternity because the Divine Craftsman always willed it to exist? In that case, how to explain the biblical account of creation from nothing, beginning at one point in time and lasting over the course of seven days? This was the question posed to the forty-two-year-old Averroës when first admitted to the court of the Almohad ruler Abu Ya'qub Yusuf. The story goes that Averroës held his tongue until the monarch had expounded on the thorny subject because he knew that the answer impinged on the Qur'an's teaching that the world had sprung from a temporal creation.[36] In the wake of his contemporary, Maimonides argued that once the theory of *creatio ab nihilo*, "creation from nothing," is found to be true, the account of Genesis can be correctly interpreted accordingly. In magnificent contradiction to some of his other arguments, Maimonides claimed that just such a seemingly inscrutable purpose would stand the test of reason.

8

◆─◆─◆

Maimonides the Believer

Hear, O Israel: The LORD our God,
the Lord is one LORD!

—Deuteronomy 6:4

BUT HOW DO YOU DISCUSS a concept that you define as essentially inscrutable? The answer, if you were a medieval Jew and a believer, must lie in the Torah. For Maimonides, only the Torah and its complement, the Talmud, were the true sources of philosophical inquiry, and for the most part Maimonides found their tenets echoed in Aristotle's metaphysics, filtered through Arab thinkers (Averroës, Al-Farabi, Avicenna). A key text in their studies was the *Theology of Aristotle*, a book that, though attributed to Aristotle by Jewish and Islamic scholars, was in fact a summary of parts of books 4 to 6 of Plotinus's *Enneads*. Certain concepts in the *Theology* were essential to the beliefs of several Islamic masters and in turn became core concepts in Maimonides' philosophy. First among them was the idea that God is a unity of pure goodness and pure being, that he is the first cause of all beings, and that he is who creates by

Mishneh Torah, copied in Spain, illuminated in Perugia ca. 1400, Jewish National and University Library of Israel, Jerusalem. The illustration on the top initial-word panel shows a man embracing a Torah scroll. In the lower margin another man is reciting the Shema (Hear, O Israel . . .) before going to bed. (Photo: The Picture Art Collection/Alamy Stock Photo)

emanation first the intellect, then the soul, then all of nature. "For our knowledge is separate from our essence, but His essence is perfect and cannot be separated from any aspect thereof," Maimonides wrote. "His knowledge and His life are One in all respects. For if His knowledge were separate, there would be a plurality in Him. . . . He is absolutely and completely One and He is our Unique One, and our Torah and our faith revolve around Him."[1]

Aristotle, following Parmenides, declared in his *Metaphysics* that "the whole material universe" is one, and "the Unity is God," and that "God is a living being, eternal, most good, and therefore life and a continuous eternal existence belong to God; for that is what God is."[2] Philo of Alexandria regarded the number 1 as God's number and the basis for all numbers.[3] For Plotinus as well, three centuries later, the One is the ultimate reality and the source of all existence. Following in their footsteps, Maimonides stated: "The Foundations of Foundation and the Pillar of all Wisdom is to know that there is a First Cause. . . . This God is one; He is neither two nor more than two. He is simply one. His unity is not like any other oneness that exists in the world. His is not the unity of a kind that encompasses many other single particulars; and it is not like the unity of a body that is divided into parts and extremities; rather it is a unity that is entirely unlike any other sort of oneness in the universe."[4] For Maimonides, God is certainly one but this oneness is entirely other, and does not partake of human time and space except as the Creator of all.

Anything in the universe, however singular it might seem, is composed of several elements, or parts, and qualities. Its singularity is therefore plural: the singular moon is made of innumerable spots and grains of dust; the singular phoenix comprises feathers and claws that will be reborn every time the unique being perishes once more in the flames. Only God is nothing but God, and only God can be said to be one. "I am who I am" says God to Moses, speaking out of the burning bush. The first person of the Hebrew verb *li-hiot*, "to be," is *ehyeh*, and according to the rules of Hebrew grammar it denotes both the future and the past tense: "I was" and "I will be." The present moment is not announced because it is already past. The singularity of God embraces every moment in time as his omnipresence occupies every point in space. The true name of God is therefore One because it can apply to nothing else but God.

To define this unique One, Maimonides proposed what has been called an apophatic or negative theology, a doctrine of negative attributes suggested already by the pre-Socratics. According to Maimonides, God cannot be described except in the negative: God is not nonexistent, or noneternal, or incapable. God is the source of all movement (the First Cause) but nothing moves him. "For I am the Lord, I change not," Maimonides quotes from Malachi 3:6.[5] God, however, cannot be supposed to indulge in logical absurdities. The Aristotelian God cannot make a thing exist and not exist at the same time. Divine logic governs him who is also that logic.

Even to speak of him is impossible: God is beyond all language. Any attempt to praise God in words diminishes our apprehension of his greatness. He is ineffable, and words limit, constrain, and oversimplify. But we can, nevertheless, see, hear, touch, smell, taste, and admire with our intellect his works. We can attempt to know him indirectly, by means of our senses, through his creation, through what we might call the proofs of his action. In this way, "we might speak meaningfully of *imitatio dei* as the human ideal."[6] With regard to God, Maimonides argues, the intellectual agents responsible for the creation of notions, the action of constructing, and the object of the action are all three identical to one another and do not exist as singularities but as the unique One, while in human beings the three are distinct and independent. In this, Maimonides is following Alexander of Aphrodisias, who defined the intellect as a mere "disposition" that receives notions from without. For Alexander, ideas are simultaneously subject, action, and object.[7] Maimonides audaciously applied Alexander's definition of ideas to God, and just as audaciously compared this trinitarian definition to "what the Christians say: namely that He is one but also three, and that the three are one."[8] Maimonides was conversant in Christian theology and the doctrine of the Trinity initiated by Theophilus of Antioch in the second century.[9] Maimonides had probably learned the tenets of Christian faith from the Coptic community in Fustat, and though there is evidence that he believed Christianity to foster idolatry, a fair number of comparative references to Christian thought appear in his writings.[10]

This possibility of knowing God's attributes (or rather, the lack thereof) was heatedly debated not only among Jewish scholars but among Islamic scholars as well, as Maimonides was certainly aware. In his *Treatise on Asthma*, he quotes Alexander as saying, "There are three causes of disagreements about things. One of them is love of dominion and love of strife, both of which turn man aside from apprehension of truth as it is. The second cause is the subtlety and obscurity of the object of apprehension in itself and the difficulty of apprehending it. And the third cause is the ignorance of him who apprehends and his inability to grasp things that it is possible to apprehend."[11] What attitude should a person take when confronted with a God who is at the same time the giver of the visible Law, and the unseeable and ineffable Presence?

A key question in the philosophical discussions, be it among Aristotle and his commentators or Maimonides' Jewish and Arab contemporaries, concerned the valid methods to explore "the subtlety and obscurity of the object of apprehension in itself." The Mutakallim, taking their cue from Aristotle, mirrored in some ways Maimonides' proposed logical strategies. The Mutakallim's purpose was to bring contradictory notions of revelation apparent in the Qur'an and the Hadith (the record of the traditions and sayings of the Prophet Muhammad) into some systematic, internal harmony. Maimonides, while disagreeing with what he saw as the Mutakallim's use of the imagination instead of the intellect, concurred with them in stressing God's unity through the essential belief that God does not have "differing notions"; once again, that God is an absolute unity without accidents or attributes.

In spite of his reverence for Aristotle, Maimonides could on occasion diverge radically from the master. For the Greeks since the time of the pre-Socratics, the soul is a principle that accounts for both change and repose in all living bodies, whether plants, animals, or human beings. The relation between soul and body is an instance of the more general relation between form and matter. The soul, according to Aristotle, does not have an existence or (perhaps more important) any kind of activity outside the body. "The soul is in the primary way that by which we live and perceive and think, so that it will be a sort of organization [*logos*] and a form, but not matter and a substrate."[12] Maimonides firmly disagrees. Body and the soul, for Maimonides, are one. The soul has five parts, each of which is responsible for a different function in the human being, and not so in other living things: "Mark this point well, for it is very important, as many so-called philosophers have fallen into error regarding it," he sternly warns his readers.[13] The soul has its home in the body and guides it from within. In this respect, God's Law aims at essentially two things: the health of the body and the improvement of the soul; in every case, the health of the former is a means of achieving that of the latter. The soul is also improved by acquiring the true knowledge of all that a human being is capable of knowing. The more knowledge the soul acquires, the better it is able to fulfill God's commandments.

A century before Maimonides, the Sepharad poet Solomon ibn Gabirol had argued that God had created the world through thought: all creation issued from the divine act of thinking, and because God's thoughts cannot be fathomed, the act of creation is forbidden to our understanding. "The First Author," Ibn Gabirol concluded, "is in all beings and nothing can exist without him."[14] Maimonides took this point farther and judged that the ultimate intention of the First Author in creating the world was the creation of the human being, and that the purpose of this particular creation is the achievement of happiness, Aristotle's summum bonum, the knowledge of God through philosophical inquiry and adherence to the Law. But (as he warns his pupil Joseph ibn 'Aknin, to whom the *Guide* is dedicated) we must beware the temptation of the contrary belief. If God created the world at a precise moment, that would mean that God changed from being a creator in potentia to an actual creator de facto: the difference between an artist at the point of conceiving a work and that same artist after the execution of the work. This would imply that God—the immutable One—had changed, or that he showed himself to be imperfect since, previous to the events described in the book of Genesis, he could have but did not create. Hence, the argument is a logical fallacy.

Maimonides' brave attempt to reconcile Genesis with Aristotle's metaphysics caused a prolonged quarrel between orthodox and more liberal-minded Jews in France and Spain, and after his death a number of orthodox Jews went as far as to brand Maimonides an unbeliever. The controversy continued well into the sixteenth century, when the Polish Talmudist Moses Isserles felt obliged to defend Maimonides from the criticism of the great halakhist Solomon Luria when the latter maintained that the Rambam should not have attempted to reconcile religion with philosophical pursuits.[15] It was not, all things considered, a devastating reproach. Most of those who disagree with Maimonides, confronted with his towering and ever-present influence, do not seem willing to criticize him directly but address their objections to certain passages of his work or blame the perceived errors on the faulty interpretations of some of his perplexed readers.

9

How Should One Live?

Lord of wondrous workings,
grant us understanding—
now and at the hour of our closing.

—Moses ibn Ezra (eleventh century)

WHEN LOOKING INTO the life of a figure such as Maimonides, someone whose ideas and personality have inspired, perplexed, and guided readers from different cultures, disciplines, and faiths across almost ten centuries, readers are faced with a bewildering tangle of learned commentaries, ingenious interpretations, and historical facts through which they must cut their way, knowing that the result of their quest will be incomplete at worst and selective at best. And yet if they persevere, they can nevertheless hope that honest admiration for the subject might allow for the discovery of an illuminating starting point from which to map, if not the entire intellectual continent, at least a small province of such a colossal spirit. Such a starting point might be an incident that took place around 1173, when Maimonides was thirty-five, almost exactly at the mid-point of his itinerant life.

In that corner of the Middle East that Ptolemy wishfully described as Arabia Felix and is now known as Yemen, during the years 1173 and 1174 Saladin's older brother Shams ad-Din Turanshah ibn Ayyub al-Malik al-Mu'azzam Shams ad-Dawla Fakhr ad-Din, his cumbersome name conveniently polished down to Turanshah, succeeded in strengthening the authority of his famous brother by conquering the rebellious Yemenite provinces. Saladin rewarded Turanshah by granting him rich estates in the Yemenite countryside, but Turanshah pined for Egypt and eventually succeeded in being appointed Ayyubid governor of Alexandria, where he died soon afterward, in 1180.

Saladin had founded the Ayyubid dynasty in 1174, shortly after being proclaimed sultan. Based on traditionalist Sunni tenets, the Ayyubid dynasty centered itself in Egypt and throughout the twelfth and thirteenth centuries held dominion over much of the eastern Arab world with its kaleidoscopic combination of ethnicities and creeds. At the time of Turanshah's campaigns, the small Jewish population of Yemen, scattered throughout the country, was allowed to live in comparative religious freedom. However, shortly after Turanshah's death, the Yemenite Shia, aided by local tribesmen inimical to Saladin, took on as their head an orthodox Shiite, the Zaydi chief 'Abd an-Nabi ibn Mahdi, who opposed the Sunnis' less restrictive ideology. Ibn Mahdi began a fierce persecution of the Yemenite Jews, forcing them, as the Almohads had done earlier in al-Andalus and North Africa, to choose between conversion to Islam or death.

The question of converting in order to save one's life was debated with anguish in the Jewish communities everywhere, under both Arab and Christian rule. The Ashkenazi halakhists sternly condemned conversion whatever the circumstances. Maimonides, who had himself experienced the quandary, proved to be more lenient. Mainly in two of his writings, the *Epistle on Conversion* and the *Mishneh Torah*, Maimonides argued that conversion is a capital offense only if the choice is not between life and death, because to submit to death in the name of God can never be a voluntary choice; no one but God can decree martyrdom. "How could the law possibly treat equally one who violates the law under duress, about whom the rabbis declared: 'Let him transgress rather than suffer death,' and one who does it wilfully?"[1]

Maimonides' *Epistle on Conversion*, while addressed to a rabbi who (in Maimonides' opinion) had given a mistaken answer to a correspondent seeking advice on the question, is intended for all Jews living under the shadow of persecution. How should one confront the threat of a forced conversion? The rabbi's correspondent had asked whether to "accept the Mohammedan confession and spare their children from falling into the hands of their oppressors, or refuse to pronounce the Islamic formula, and suffer martyrdom—a fate presumably prescribed by the laws of Moses."[2] The rabbi, agreeing with the conflicted correspondent that there were only two choices in this dilemma, advised martyrdom, arguing that those who agreed to convert to save their lives were irredeemable sinners.

Maimonides' answer is twofold. The rabbi was mistaken in giving an answer that "brought darkness into the heart of men." "*He sent darkness; it was very dark!*" Maimonides quotes from the book of Psalms (105:28). If one is obliged to break any of the commandments related to idolatry, incest, or bloodshed, one must accept death rather than transgress: "There are no exceptions to this ruling." But concerning all other commandments that the Jew might be forced to transgress in order to save his life, Maimonides' opinion is quite as adamant: "The Jew is to transgress and not choose death." The reason Maimonides gives for this judgment is that conversion undertaken under threat of death is invalid. He asks, "Suppose the practise of heathen worshippers entailed the sacrifice of children as burnt offerings, should we, therefore, emulate them and act likewise in the service of our God?"[3] Maimonides put his answer in terms of an affirmation of what he considered the primary obligation of a human being: to preserve human life at all costs. The King James version has God say to Moses: "Ye shall therefore keep my statutes, and my judgments: which if a man do, he shall live in them" (Leviticus 18:5). God, Maimonides points out, specifically said "he shall *live* in them," not "shall *die* in them."

And yet Maimonides understood that the circumstances of each case were different and should therefore be judged accordingly. In many cases, Jews had been forced to convert on pain of death, all the while secretly keeping their true faith in their hearts, and this, Maimonides thought, should undoubtedly be considered when judging their conduct.

In other cases, as in that of certain North African Jewish martyrs who had accepted death rather than abjure their faith, Maimonides argued that their suffering should be acknowledged and leniency applied to their acceptance of death. However, Maimonides, the practical man, advised that if at all possible, the best action to take in the face of persecution was to emigrate. Using his own family's enforced exile as an example, and with Moses' exodus from Egypt in mind, Maimonides writes, "However, the crucial advice I wish to give to myself and to those I admire and to those who seek my opinion is to leave those places of hostility and go to a location where one could fulfill the Law without compulsion or fear."[4] As generations of Jews up to our time have learned, Maimonides' optimism has never been fully justified.

In such a bleak political climate, the Jews of Yemen were faced with yet another challenge, this time from within their fold. A Jewish preacher, whose name has not been confidently established but calling himself the True Messiah, announced to the Jewish communities that the Holy Book, the Torah, if read properly—that is, radically reinterpreted—proclaimed in veiled terms the advent of Islam and of the Prophet Muhammad, and that it was therefore the duty of all Jews to convert to the Islamic faith.[5] One of the Jewish leaders of Yemen, Rabbi Ya'akov al-Fayyumi, troubled by this revelation and uncertain as to what to instruct his brethren, decided to write a letter to Maimonides, who was then residing in Egypt, seeking his advice. In his letter, Rabbi Ya'akov asked Maimonides what the proper behavior was for a Jew in the face of such perplexing uncertainties, and whether these present tribulations were not perhaps due to the influence of the unappealable stars.

Maimonides was overworked and much solicited, but he answered carefully and at length. His letter to Rabbi Ya'akov, written in Judeo-Arabic and later translated into Hebrew, was to have a powerful and long-lasting effect on the Jewish population of Yemen, and also abroad. Though not a major work like the *Mishneh Torah* or the *Guide*, the text known as *Iggeret Teiman* in Hebrew, *Petah Tiqwa* in Judeo-Arabic, and *Epistle to Yemen* in English exemplifies Maimonides' essential beliefs, both social and religious.

Maimonides was aware that his ideas were largely conditioned by the circumstances of his wandering life, the life of an exile and a refugee, like that of Ovid before him and Dante after him. With a touch of unwarranted modesty (his *excusatio propia infirmitatis*, the confession of his own weakness, a rhetorical device common in the literature of the Middle Ages) Maimonides begins his letter by declaring himself to be "one of the humblest scholars of Spain whose prestige is low in exile. I am always dedicated to my duties, but have not attained the learning of my forebears, for evil days and hard times have overtaken us and we have not lived in tranquility; we have labored without finding rest. How can the Law become lucid to a fugitive from city to city, from country to country?"[6]

After praising the Jews of Yemen for their strict adherence

to the Law and for their scholarly wisdom, Maimonides sternly advises Rabbi Ya'akov to "expunge from his heart" the absurd superstitions of astrology and the impious notion that the constellations influence our conduct, and recommends the position to adopt against the preaching of the false Messiah. Maimonides decries the reputed powers of astrology, but at the same time, as a true scholar he had read and mastered the canonical texts of this pseudo-science and so was able to back his arguments with academic precision.

"When your letter reached us in Egypt," Maimonides continues, "all ears were pleased to hear it, as was it desirable [also] to the sight. It bore witness before us concerning you, that you are of the servants of the Lord who dwell in His quarter, who are encamped beside His banner, and who are of those who pursue [diligently] the [divine] Law, and those who love its commissions, [even] those who attend fervently at its doors."[7]

Maimonides deals curtly with the question of the supposed Messiah. The arguments of this "madman," Maimonides says, "have been rehearsed so often that they have become nauseating. It is not enough to declare that they are altogether feeble; nay, to cite them as proofs is ridiculous and absurd in the extreme." Maimonides then adopts the voice of a philological scholar and teacher. "Under the circumstances it is incumbent upon you to concentrate and understand what I am about to say. Remember that it is not right to take a passage out of its context and argue from it. . . . No text can possibly be cited as evidence before the aim of the author and its context are grasped." And after demolishing through logical arguments the pretenses of the false Messiah, Maimonides concludes that it is not enough to clarify the mistakes of the old; the young should be instructed in the tenets of the truth, "because they are a pillar of our faith."[8] He then proceeds to explain how these tenets should be taught.

In order to put the question into historical context, Maimonides lists what he considers the three traditional opponents of the Jewish faith, appearing in varying guises throughout time. First, the system of coercion of the ancient enslavers of the Jews, such as Nebuchadnezzar and Titus. Second, the system of sophistry, present, for all its other fundamental and true values, in the charms of pagan thought (what in our time Cynthia Ozick would call "idolatry"). Third, the false pretenders to divine privilege, followers of Christ and Muhammad. These latter ones, closer as we know to Maimonides' Sepharad heart, might enjoy prosperity for a certain time but their glory will prove ephemeral, as the Lord has decreed.

However, the faithful Jews who "pursue the divine Law" are not, Maimonides goes on to say, the majority. Jews have misbehaved ever since the first transgression in the Garden of Eden. From Adam on, Jews have broken the Law and displeased God, as all the prophets have loudly proclaimed. In the case of Adam, the sin was disobedience; in the case of Noah, it was negligence, which caused him to become drunk after the Flood. Later, when Nebuchadnezzar captured Jerusalem in 586 BCE and destroyed the Temple of Solomon, and after that, in 70 CE, when the Romans took the city and destroyed the Second Temple, the sin for which the Jews were punished was idolatry (though a cause often cited is "baseless hatred").[9] The nature of their sin changed through time but they were always pardoned by God's infinite mercy. And yet, in spite of his constant forgiveness, the Jews continued to sin against him. For that reason, again and again, the Jews had to be instructed in what it meant to be Jewish and how to keep the Law according to God's will. They had to be admonished to remember not to forget. Maimonides understood that his mission was to remind his people of what was once taught to them and what they so many times let fall into oblivion, and help them on the way to renewed enlightenment.

10

Lessons from Exodus

If thou shalt do this thing, and God command thee
so, then thou shalt be able to endure, and all this
people shall also go to their place in peace.

—Exodus 18:23

IN THE QUR'AN it is stated, "We shall show them Our signs
in every region of the earth and in themselves until it becomes
clear to them that this is the Truth. Is it not enough that your
Lord witnesses everything?" (41:53). The mystic philosopher
Ibn 'Arabi, a near contemporary of Maimonides and a fellow
Andalusian, believed that these signs could be read not through
reason but rather through divine inspiration (akin to Aristotle's
phantasia). "Knowledge—every knowledge—is gained through
a signifying, because *'ilm* [knowledge] is derived from *'alama*
[mark]. That is why knowledge of the things is attributed to
God, for He knows Himself, and thereby He knows the cosmos. Hence He is both a signifier and a mark of the cosmos. In
a similar way, the cosmos is a mark of Him in our knowledge
of Him. This is indicated by the Prophet's words, 'He who

knows himself knows his Lord.' Hence He made you your signifier of Him, and you came to know Him. Likewise, His Essence is His signifier of you, so He knew you and then brought
you into existence."[1] God, as the Question Mark, created his
questioner.

In the second chapter of his *Guide of the Perplexed*, Maimonides argued that Adam must have possessed perfect metaphysical knowledge, a knowledge that must have included belief in
God as an immutable and immaterial being set outside time.[2]
Scrutinizing the Bible for scriptural evidence, Maimonides explained that he had found it in the book of Kings and the book
of Wars (a lost book referred to in Numbers 21:14 ff). However,
Adam's primordial divine knowledge was lost during the time
of Enosh, the first grandson of Adam, discovered once more by
Abraham, passed down to Isaac and Jacob, and then lost again
during the time of the captivity in Egypt, when the Jews fell
prey to the pagan beliefs of their Egyptian masters.[3] The Torah
warns in unequivocal terms, "Take care lest you forget the
Lord your God and fail to keep His commandments, His rules,
and His laws . . . you shall certainly perish" (Deuteronomy 8:11,
19). And yet, again and again the Jews forgot, and again and
again a handful of virtuous sages took it upon themselves to remind the Jews of what they had forgotten. The history of the
Jews can be seen as a history of learning and forgetting, bound
to an epistemological Mobius strip that will come to an end
only on the Day of Judgment.

From the point of view of most historiographers, Maimonides was not a historian.[4] For Maimonides, historical progress
is, at its best, a deepening of learning, not a progressive accu-
mulation of discoveries and insights, because truth is essentially
unchangeable. "Hear the truth from whoever utters it," he says
in the introduction to one of his Talmudic commentaries, probably bearing in mind versions of the truth found in his Greek
and Arab readings.[5] Only the arrival of the Messiah will allow

humankind to see the truth as the prophets saw it, and establish a universal climate of study and reflection. But for the majority of the Jews, with few exceptions (such as Josephus, in his chronicle of the Jewish War), history was not the sequence of events that the rest of the world painfully chronicled but certain remembered exemplary moments that belonged to the same coeval place and time from which lessons could be learned, and their causes found in the Torah.

Maimonides believed that everything in the Torah was set out for the purpose of keeping the Jewish people together: everything, down to the style and the narrative sequence. For example, the abrupt thematic changes in the Torah narration, the repetitions and seeming contradictions, the different tones and many voices, were not due to the fact of their having been composed by diverse anonymous hands (as some scholars suggested) but were deliberate narrative strategies, and they held an occult divine meaning, as expressed in Proverbs 25:11: "Like golden apples in silver showpieces / Is a phrase well turned."

In many cases, the "phrase well turned" is submitted by Maimonides to an etymological scrutiny. Words such as *serpent* in the story of the Garden of Eden or *satan* in the story of Job, cannot claim "true realities of existence" and therefore should be understood as figures of speech, metaphors or symbols befitting the style of the narrative.[6] For instance, the word *satan*, Maimonides explains, "derives from [the verb "satah," to turn away, figuring for instance in the verse]: *Steh [turn away] from him and pass on* [Proverbs 4:15]. I mean to say that it derives from the notion of turning-away and going-away. For it is he who indubitably turns people away from the ways of truth and makes them perish in the ways of error."[7] In other chapters of the *Guide*, Maimonides provides further aspects of meaning, suggesting that he did not believe in the actual existence of a being called Satan but thought instead that the name should read as a symbol of evil.

For Maimonides the philosopher, the completeness of the Torah meant that every word in it must have at least two facets, one exterior and the other interior: the exterior for use in social communication, the interior in the lifelong search for the hidden truths set forth therein. In pre-Maimonidean Jewish philosophy, it was stated that there existed a rational process, independent of tradition or revelation, "for gaining knowledge of God, the world, and morality."[8] Maimonides heartily agreed. Reason, according to Maimonides, would allow the enlightened seeker to discover empirically whether a statement that according to factual evidence and also to faith must be true were indeed true. In this semantic interpretation of the sacred text, Maimonides anticipates the two-dimensional (2D) semantic theories of the 1970s that proposed formal frameworks to determine the meaning of certain linguistic expressions and the relation between the sentences containing them—that is to say, between the actual sense of a word and the truth of the sentence that contains it, whether as a factual statement or intended as a metaphor or allegory. In Maimonides' view, both the Torah that "will not be changed"[9] and the Talmud in all its practical dialectical wisdom were written deliberately in this allusive style, as an admission of the feebleness inherent in every one of us, their readers.

11

The Talmud

The reason that the Talmud lacks a first page
is that however many pages the studious man reads,
he must never forget that he has not yet reached
the very first page.

—Rabbi Levi Yitzhak of Berdichev
(eighteenth century)

THE CREATION of the Talmud remains a mystery. Tradition says that the Oral Law was revealed by God to Moses on Mount Sinai, and that Moses transmitted it orally to Joshua, and Joshua to the heads of the Jewish congregations, and they to their successors. The text of the Talmud as a whole appears to the unenlightened eye an arbitrary succession of convoluted opinions and inferences that seem to be governed by no coherent principle, split into two arbitrary sections: the oral laws and rabbinical notes (the Mishnah) and their discussion (the Gemara). This apparent randomness merits consideration.

The Mishnah itself, being mainly concerned with halakhic

matters, is written in a deliberately terse and clear style, as if intended for the common reader. However, since much in legal matters depends on interpretation, rabbinical commentators engaged among themselves and with their students in a learned dialogue to analyze and discuss the Mishnah, whose contents were deemed incontrovertible. The result of their questions and proposed answers, and the opinions on those answers and questions, spanned three centuries, from the third to the sixth, and constitutes the main corpus of the Talmud.

"If the Bible is the cornerstone of Judaism," wrote the eminent Talmudist Adin Steinsaltz, "then the Talmud is the central pillar, soaring from the foundations and supporting the entire spiritual and intellectual edifice."[1] The Talmud was not conceived as a text to be read as literature or as a sourcebook for preaching or scholarly discourse. It resembles lecture notes or minutes of a learned conversation that stretches over hundreds of years. The Talmud deals with everything, both the totality of things, collectively and individually, and their particular nature in accordance with the Torah. Its apparent disorder disguises an associative methodology, a system conceived by a mind simultaneously rational and imaginative, capable of finding similarities in disparate things, and common questions on a variety of subjects.

The matter of the Talmud is further complicated by there being not one but two Talmuds: that of Babylon, compiled in Babylonian Jewish-Aramaic between the third to sixth centuries and revised by generations of rabbinical scholars, and the Jerusalem Talmud (though it was not produced in Jerusalem but in other cities of Roman Palestine), written in Palestinian-Aramaic and left incomplete at the end of the fifth century. Though both are based on the Mishnah, the two Talmuds present notable differences. For example, the Jerusalem Talmud, fragmentary and often difficult to read, deals in part with laws concerning specific aspects of the Palestinian region, and in-

The Copenhagen *Moreh Nebukhim* (*Guide of the Perplexed*), Codex XXXVIII, Fol. 114. The illumination shows a group of people involved in discussion with a seated man who holds a gold astrolabe while his left hand rests on an open book. (Royal Danish Library).

cludes certain questions concerning the Haggadah (Seder readings) that are not present in the Babylonian one. The Babylonian Talmud, on the other hand, discusses, for instance, the Mishnaic order of Kodashim that deals with sacrificial rites and laws pertaining to the Temple of Jerusalem, a subject that is not present in the Jerusalem Talmud. The word *Talmud*, when used without qualification, usually refers to the Babylonian one.

The Talmud can be understood as the contrary of a catechism or universal dogma, but that does not mean that the knowledge derived from studying it need not be acted upon in the reader's place and time. A Talmudic scholar should serve as a living example of the Talmud's truth. Because the search for this truth is never-ending, the Talmud is largely written in the interrogative mode. As regards the Talmud, says Steinsaltz, "doubt is not only legitimate, but an essential strategy for the advancement of learning."[2] The Talmud urges its readers not to take anything for granted. Since absolute certainty can rarely be reached, the Talmud allows for a vast field of discussion, argument, and counterargument, in an attempt to sharpen increasingly the logical conclusions. "From this point of view," Steinsaltz says, "the Talmud is perhaps the only sacred book in all of world culture that permits and even encourages the student to question it."[3]

An old Jewish joke exemplifies this ongoing, dialectical exchange between the Talmudic commentators and the common reader, demanding from all participants at the same time keen logic, admission of a priori and a posteriori arguments, and solid common sense.

A Gentile met a rabbi and said to him, "You have taught me many things but there is one thing in particular I want to learn very much but you do not wish to teach to me. I want you to teach me the Talmud." The rabbi replied, "You are a non-Jew and you have the brain of a non-Jew. There is no chance that you will succeed in understanding the Talmud." But the Gentile continued in his attempt to persuade the rabbi to teach him the Talmud. Finally, the rabbi agreed. The rabbi then said to the Gentile, "I agree to teach you the Talmud on condition that you answer one question." The Gentile agreed and asked the rabbi, "What is the question?" The rabbi then said to the Gentile, "Two men fall down through the chimney. One comes out dirty and the other comes out clean. Who of those two goes to wash up?" "Very simple," replied the Gentile. "The one who is dirty goes to wash up but the one who is clean does not go to wash up." The rabbi then said to the Gentile, "I told you that you would not succeed in understanding the Talmud. The exact opposite happened. The clean one looks at the dirty one and thinks that he is also dirty and goes to wash up. The dirty one, on the other hand, looks at the clean one and thinks that he is also clean and therefore does not go to wash up." The Gentile said to the rabbi, "This I did not think of. Ask me, please, another question." The rabbi then said to the Gentile, "Two men fall down through the chimney. One comes out dirty and the other comes out clean. Who of these two goes to wash up?" The Gentile replied to the rabbi, "Very simple. The clean one looks at the dirty one and thinks he is also dirty and goes to wash up. The dirty one, on the other hand, looks at the clean one and thinks that he is also clean and therefore does not go to wash up." The rabbi said to the Gentile, "You are wrong again. I told you that you would not understand. The clean one looks into the mirror, sees that he is clean, and therefore does not go to wash up. The dirty one looks into the mirror, sees that he is dirty, and goes to wash up." The Gentile complained to the rabbi, "But you did not tell me that that there was a mirror there." The rabbi said to the Gentile, "I said that you were a non-Jew, and that with your brain you would not succeed in understanding the Talmud. According to the Talmud, you have to think of all the possibilities." "All right," groaned the Gentile to the Rabbi. "Let us try once more. Ask me one more question." For the last time, the rabbi said to the Gentile, "Two men fall through the chimney. One came out dirty and the other came out clean. Who of these two went to wash up?" "That is very simple!" replied the Gentile. "If there is no mirror there the clean one will look at the dirty one and will think that he is also dirty and will therefore go to wash up. The dirty one will look at the clean one and will think that he is also clean and will therefore not go to wash up. If there is a mirror there, the clean one will look into the mirror and will see that he is clean and will therefore not go to wash up. The dirty one will look into the mirror and will see that he is dirty and will therefore go to wash up." The rabbi said to the Gentile, "I told you that you would not succeed in understanding. You are a non-Jew, you have a non-Jewish brain. Tell me, how is it possible for two men to fall through a chimney and for one to come out dirty and for the other to come out clean?"

Maimonides, undertaking both in his *Commentary on the Mishnah* and in his *Mishneh Torah* the enormous project of commenting on the entire legal Jewish corpus, states briefly his intended procedure: to transcribe all the words of the Mishnah "up until the end of the Law," and then to discuss the explanation of those laws. "I continue so until the end of the Mishnah. Each law which is well-known and whose meaning is self-evident, I will merely record, and it will be unnecessary to comment upon it." And he adds, "Our commentary is not intended to instruct stones, but to inform him who has the heart to understand."[4] Comparing the Talmud to "a Daedalian maze in which one can hardly find one's way even with the thread of Ariadne," the nineteenth-century German historian Heinrich Graetz called Maimonides' *Mishneh Torah* "a well-contrived ground plan, with wings, halls, apartments, and chambers, through which a stranger might pass without a guide."[5]

12

The Law

Why are matters of Torah compared to fire . . . ?
To tell you: Just as fire does not ignite in a lone stick
of wood but in a pile of kindling, so too, matters of
Torah are not retained and understood properly
by a lone scholar who studies by himself,
but by a group of Sages.

—Taanit 7a

EVER SINCE the first stirrings of a people that defined themselves as Jewish, Jews have lived, and today continue to live, in
constant fear of persecution. Job's question "Should we accept
only good from God and not accept evil?" (Job 2:10) seems to
suffice as an answer for many in the face of injustice, but for
others, another deeply human question remains: "Why do these
things happen to us, God's chosen people? Why does God not
hear our prayers?" In this light, Job can be considered the first
of the perplexed, the ideal recipient of Maimonides' *Guide* (the
patient endurer whom Maimonides discusses in the third part

of the book). Job has erred intellectually, though not practically, putting in doubt God's infallible providence and not understanding that God's gift was all-encompassing, that it entailed both good and evil consequences, and that our obligation was to decide how to behave when faced with either.[1]

As a Jew, Maimonides had learned that wherever the Jewish people "made in God's image" chose to settle, their security could not be entrusted to either their non-Jewish neighbors or the local authorities. They needed to secure protection from the highest authority available, a "direct vertical alliance" with whoever was the head of state. "In bypassing lower and local jurisdiction," writes the historian Yosef Hayim Yerushalmi, "Jews both gained and lost. If the central authority was prone to regard them as natural allies, by that very token they further aroused the resentment of an already hostile populace. The more the Jews sought protection of the former, the more they found themselves in tension with the latter, and so each trend reinforced the other in a seemingly endless spiral. It was, on the whole, one of the more tragic aspects of the dialectics of Jewish existence among the nations."[2] The only trustworthy authority was that of he who is one. So why did he not protect his people?

In a treatise attributed to Maimonides but now proved to be an abbreviated version of the 1615 Kabbalistic text *Ginnat Egoz* by Rabbi Joseph Gikatilla, the question is stated in this way: "What benefit is there in crying out [to God] in our troubles since He does not change after supplication from what that which preceded the supplication?"[3] Change, the author of the treatise answers, depends not on the unchangeable deity but on us, whose supplications are meant to purify our souls and draw us nearer to God. Prayer is confession, not a demand for change, in order to reach an ideal state of obedience to the One. Confession, however, might lead to change, but only if that is the will of God.

George Steiner, in one of his Yale lectures, attempted to

explain the age-old worldwide anti-Semitic prejudice by suggesting that it arose as a response to the Jewish people's introduction, several millennia ago, of the notion of "Ideal" into Western culture. According to Steiner, Hitler's accusation that the Jews "invented consciousness" explains, at least in part, the persistent hatred of the Jews and their consequent persecution.[4] Until the time of Moses, the different civilizations of the world had grappled with the multifarious universe presented to their senses by means of a variety of narratives of miraculous creations and divine incarnations. Whether in Greece, Egypt, China, or the South Seas, people told the tales of numberless divinities that in a time before time fashioned the world or caused it to come into being, after which they themselves or newer gods took residence in their creation. A multiplicity of immortal creatures watched over humankind or threatened it, and nothing existed that did not carry the imprint of a god, whether each of the stars and each of the winds, every flower and every bird. Visible or invisible, the gods could speak in an intelligible tongue, could adopt any form they chose, were prey to passions and desires like the humans, and sometimes proved not to be immortal after all and died in a thunderous Götterdämmerung.

The Mosaic Law, with its idealistic concepts and ethical imperatives, "tore up the human psyche by its most ancient roots," says Steiner, doing away not just with the material gods and the multiple images of their tangible presence, through commandments against idolatry and pluralistic worship, but also with "natural sensory consciousness" and "instinctual polytheistic and animist needs."[5] Jews exchanged the sensual gratification of the material senses in earlier cultures for the purity and measured life they heard in God's commandments.

The great moment of change is described in the book of Exodus, when Moses descends from Mount Sinai after forty days and forty nights to find his people worshipping a false idol. Fearing that Moses would not return, the Jews had demanded that Aaron, Moses' elder brother, make them a deity that they could worship to alleviate their distress during their march toward the Promised Land. To satisfy their pleas, Aaron had them gather all their gold, and fashioned out of it a Golden Calf, and the people said, "This is your god, O Israel, who brought you out of the land of Egypt!"[6] Finding the people making burnt offerings to the false divinity, Moses became angry, threw down the Tablets of the Law (which broke), threw the Golden Calf into the fire, ground it to powder, scattered it on water, and forced the Jews to drink it (Exodus 32:4–24). The old gods were then subsumed into the only true Godhead whose name—Elohim—can be read as plural (as we have noted earlier) though Maimonides argued that Elohim (the One) and Elohim (the multiple deity) were homonyms. In the process, the One shed all sensorial and physical attributes to become a singular wholeness and simply be.

According to Steiner, the monotheistic religion of the Jews represents the earliest celebration of an Absolute that demands abstract precepts and material self-denial: the story of Abraham's willingness to sacrifice his son, Isaac, followed by the last-minute substitution of a sacrificial ram for Isaac, is the most savage example of this new concept—the horror of a father obeying the divine order to murder his son loses for the modern reader nothing of its repulsiveness, even after the anthropological explanation that sees in the story a passage from human sacrifices to that of animals. This injunction to replace the many ancient and concrete gods with a metaphysical One was later reclaimed by the first Christians, and later still the singularity was lost in the multiplicity of Catholic calendar saints.

Maimonides, however, seems not to have been concerned with the question Why us? Perhaps because his intellectual starting point was the utter acceptance of God's existence as the One in whom omniscience and eternity are the same concept, whose will fashioned time and the events in time, and also his creatures as inhabitants of time, Maimonides felt that to ask why bad things happen is to question God's knowledge and his sense of justice. This, in essence, is the contents of Maimonides' *Thirteen Principles*, distilled from the 613 precepts of Jewish Law, principles that according to Maimonides constituted "the fundamental truths of our religion and its very foundations."[7] Maimonides was barely in his thirties when he composed the *Thirteen Principles of Faith*. To this day, many Jewish congregations around the world recite daily Maimonides' *Thirteen Principles* (in a slightly poeticized version known as the *Yigdal*) at the end of the morning prayers.

The *Thirteen Principles* begin with the declaration "I believe with perfect faith that God is the Creator and Ruler of all things. He alone has made, does make, and will make all things": all things, both good and evil, set in a continuum of time that includes simultaneously past, present, and future.[8] Careful not to anthropomorphize or define God through external qualities, Maimonides concentrated instead on understanding his commandments. "Why is this happening?" in Maimonides' mind became "How should I respond?"

Commenting on the book of Job, Maimonides considers how misfortunes of various kinds affect people in various ways. "For some people are not frightened by the loss of their fortune and hold it a small thing, but are horrified by the death of their children and die because of their grief. Others support with patience and without terror even the loss of their children, but no one endowed with sensation can support pain patiently." When the many misfortunes mentioned in Job befall these people, "some of them become unbelievers and believe that there is little order in all that exists at the time when they lose their fortune; others hold to the belief in justice and in order in spite even of their having been stricken by the loss of their fortune, but do not keep patient if tried by the loss of their children."

All ask the wrong questions and forget the all-important caveat of God to Satan in the story: do what you will with Job, *"only spare his soul."* "This," Maimonides sternly notes, "is the thing over which *Satan* has no dominion."[9] This, a Jew must unfailingly believe.

The French medievalist Étienne Gilson reminded his readers that for Maimonides, Judaism was "first of all a religion," and "a religion is not based on liberty of thought, but upon a free acceptance of a certain way of thinking"; "one is perfectly free not to accept this way of thinking, but . . . one is not free to repudiate it, if one pretends to profess that religion."[10]

Maimonides argued that any Jew who did not hold to all thirteen principles he laid out was a heretic "and we are obligated to hate him and destroy him."[11] He proposed five categories of heretics (*minim*) which included, first, those who believed there was no God; second, those who did not believe that God was one; third, those who lent God a material body; fourth, those who believed that God did not create the world from nothing; and fifth, those who worshipped the stars, the sin of idolatry. With his five categories of heretics, Maimonides excluded from the truly faithful many well-known rabbis who spoke of God as a corporeal being and imagined that they could read God's will in astrological charts. This was a daring and dangerous proclamation.

Besides performing as a physician, philosopher, and teacher, Maimonides saw his mission as that of teaching and explaining the Torah, in order, as already noted, to keep the people together. A proper understanding of the Torah could, he believed, help solve the great questions of faith that afflicted Jewish scholars, torn as they were between the assurance of being the chosen people and the constant injustices to which they were prey. "I believe," reads his ninth principle of faith, "with perfect faith that this Torah will not be changed, and there will never be another given by God."[12] The Torah, therefore, contained the key to these anguished questions.

But how should the Torah be studied? According to Maimonides, scholarly knowledge and insight began to deteriorate almost immediately after the completion of the Talmud in the sixth century and now had to be reclaimed and relearned. In his introduction to the *Mishneh Torah*, Maimonides says, "[At the time] an extraordinarily great dispersion of Israel throughout the world took place. The people emigrated to remote parts and distant isles. The prevalence of wars and the march of armies made travel insecure. The study of the Torah declined. The Jewish people did not flock to the colleges in their thousands and tens of thousands as heretofore. . . . In our days, severe vicissitudes prevail, and all feel the pressure of hard times. The wisdom of our wise men has disappeared; the understanding of our prudent men is hidden."[13]

Faced with the despair, the doubt, and the uncertainty of the Jewish people regarding their very existence, Maimonides saw as their only hopeful source of strength the perseverance of the Torah from the time of Moses to their day and beyond, opening and closing its pages to its manifold readers. "Maimonides," notes the American scholar Alfred L. Ivry, "probably saw himself as Moses' confidant, discreetly revealing to the philosophically initiated few the truths that Moses received, but that he transmitted in popular language that often cloaked their real meaning."[14] Under that epistemological cloak, Maimonides argued, lay the one true fact that promised the Jews a key to the apparent chaotic absurdity of the world. The Almighty had given this key to his chosen people so that a truly thoughtful mind might recognize in the infallible words of the Torah a handbook which, if read properly, would lay out a map to guide us through our mapless universe. If the Almighty caused life to appear, as a deliberate and not random act, surely he would not allow his creation to wander aimlessly toward an unknown end.

Time and its imaginary linear conceptions, space and its illu-
sory sense of order and direction, take us through life, but to
find meaning on this path the Almighty (if he is not, as he must
not be by definition, unjust) cannot have sent humankind off
into his world blind, deaf, and dumb.

The all-encompassing nature of the Torah, a fundamental
pre-assumption in Maimonides' thought, is discussed in the
Zohar, a foundational Kabbalistic text that first appeared in
al-Andalus in the thirteenth century under the name of Moisés
de León, who in turn ascribed the work to the second-century
rabbi Shimon bar Yochai (known as Rashbi). Rashbi, together
with his son Eleazar, is supposed to have been taught the secrets of the Torah by the prophet Elijah himself. The Zohar
explains that "everything is found in the Torah. The Torah reveals that hidden matter and immediately it is cloaked in another garment wherein it is concealed and not revealed. But
even though the matter is hidden in its garment, the wise, who
are full of eyes, see it from within."[15] Though various legends
recount that Maimonides became interested in the Kabbalah at
the end of his life, scholars have variously denied this miraculous "conversion." What may seem anticipatory echoes in some
of Maimonides' writings of passages of the Zohar (which was
not written until decades after Maimonides' death) may perhaps
be put down to inspired coincidence.[16]

At the end of the thirteenth century, the study of the Zohar
flourished in Provence and Spain, and Kabbalistic studies spread
throughout other Jewish circles in the following centuries. Many
scholars sought to bring Maimonides' writings into their fold
and enlist the Rambam's posthumous support. Our thinking
progresses through opposition: a sense of comfort in our daily
life may breed nightmares of need in our sleep; existential anguish might provoke dreams of quiet reason. Job's unjustified
afflictions demand a logical theology that attempts to structure
and contain the tangles of unreasonable victimhood. Heinrich

Graetz suggested that the flowering of Kabbalistic writing in the thirteenth century was just such a reaction to Maimonides' rationalist demands. Graetz wrote that "it can justly be said that Judaism owes its regeneration to the thoughts of Maimonides."[17] Certain scholars of the Kabbalah, however, among them the great scholar of Jewish mysticism Gershom Scholem, found Graetz's enthusiasm overly simplistic and rejected the idea of a Kabbalistic Maimonides.

Is the Torah a premonitory record of Jewish history and of the persecutions and evil misfortunes attendant on Jews throughout the centuries? Did it accuse humankind of unending willful wickedness? Maimonides thought the question was far more complicated. He believed that the Torah, as God's gift to humankind, stemmed from his goodness because "nothing that is evil descends from above."[18] All evil is an expression of God's love which we deem evil because we do not know how to read it properly, due to our deficient capacity for apprehension; the particulars of the cause of evil acts are too intricate for the human intellect to follow. However, humans are guilty of evil acts. Aristotle had argued that every physical object is a compound of matter (*hule*) and form (*morphe*), the doctrine of hylomorphism, which was very influential in the development of medieval philosophy.[19] "All man's acts of disobedience and sins," says Maimonides, "are consequent upon his matter and not upon his form, whereas all his virtues are consequent upon his form." And Maimonides concludes by saying that the true work of God is all good, since it is existence.[20]

The Torah records all our deeds, good and evil, and Maimonides believed that good and evil were not demonstrable or even intuited intelligibles. Adam and Eve, for example, eating the forbidden fruit, committed an evil deed by allowing themselves to be distracted from intellectual activity and seeking satisfaction in the lesser objects of the imagination. "If man knows this," Maimonides wrote, "every misfortune will be borne lightly by him. And misfortunes will not add to his doubts regarding the deity and whether He does or does not know and whether He exercises providence or manifests neglect, but will, on the contrary, add to his love, as is said in the conclusion of the prophetic revelation in question: *Wherefore I abhor myself, and repent of dust and ashes* [Job 42:6]." [21]

Aristotle argued that our collective evil falls under the jurisdiction of God's will, since Divine Providence guides humanity as a whole, but it does not guide our individual acts because God's knowledge is limited to the universal. If the Godhead had knowledge of particulars, Aristotle argued, he would be subject to constant changes, and he is, by definition, immutable. Maimonides refused to attribute to God this piecemeal knowledge and insisted on God's comprehension of everything at all times as a whole. God, he says, "has known all the things that are produced anew before they have come about and . . . has known them perpetually. For this reason no new knowledge comes to Him in any way. For, seeing that He knows that a certain man is now nonexistent [i.e., has not yet been born], but will exist at a certain time, will go on existing for such and such a duration, and will then again become nonexistent, there will be for him no additional knowledge when that individual comes into existence as He had known beforehand." [22]

The Talmud states, "All that a mature disciple will yet expound before his master has already been told to Moses at Sinai." [23] History is therefore already laid out for us in the Torah, from the events that have taken place according to the biblical narration and also in our own beleaguered present, for us to decipher, all the way to the future that promises the arrival of the Messiah. These three moments are coetaneous, because it is told that "the Messiah was born the day that the Temple was destroyed." [24] In the mind of the Almighty, Maimonides believed, the end of our history marks also our beginning.

13

The Mishneh Torah

Man can, indeed, act contrarily to the decrees of God,
as far as they have been written like laws in the minds
of ourselves or the prophets, but against that eternal
decree of God, which is written in universal nature,
and has regard to the course of nature as a whole,
he can do nothing.

—Baruch Spinoza, *Political Treatise*, chap. 2,
"Of Natural Right" (1677)

DURING THE ERRATIC EXILE with his family in North Africa,
between the years 1159 and 1165, Maimonides had found time
to compose the *Commentary on the Mishnah*, finishing it in 1168.
Written in Judeo-Arabic, Maimonides' work was intended as
both an introduction and a reexamination of the Talmud, the
first extensive commentary since that of Rashi in the eleventh
century. Rashi's commentary, which only briefly addresses the
Mishnah, still appears today, side by side with the main text, in
every edition of the Babylonian Talmud, as established in the

Mishneh Torah, Fol. 85v, attributed to Master of the Barbo Missal (Italian), ca. 1457, showing the preparation for the Passover meal. (Jointly owned by The Israel Museum, Jerusalem, and The Metropolitan Museum of Art, New York, 2013. Purchased for the Israel Museum through the generosity of an anonymous donor; René and Susanne Braginsky, Zurich; Renée and Lester Crown, Chicago; Schusterman Foundation—Israel; and Judy and Michael Steinhardt, New York. Purchased for The Metropolitan Museum of Art with Director's Funds and Judy and Michael Steinhardt Gift. Photo © The Israel Museum, by Ardon Bar-Hama.)

first layout designed by the Flemish printer Daniel Bomberg in Venice in 1519. Rashi's words were considered essential; Maimonides intended to reach even further, digging more deeply into the text and addressing a wider readership.

Maimonides' *Commentary* is remarkable not only for its close textual annotation and conceptual analysis but for its many original philosophical and scientific comments, dealing with the doctrinal foundations of the Oral Law, as well as the ethical notion of virtue according to Aristotle's golden mean. Maimonides translated Aristotle's fundamental concept into Jewish ethical terms: "Good deeds are such as are equibalanced, maintaining the mean between two equally bad extremes. . . . Virtues are psychic conditions and dispositions which are midway between two reprehensible extremes."[1]

Three sections in particular deserve close attention. The first is the "General Introduction," which addresses the importance of homiletic exposition. The second is his "Introduction to the Tractate Avot," known as *Eight Chapters*. The third is the "Commentary on the Tractate Sanhedrin," which discusses the tenets of the Jewish religion. In this last section, Maimonides listed what he judged to be the basic principles of faith, the *Thirteen Precepts* previously mentioned.

The *Commentary on the Mishnah* can be seen as precursory work for the great reordering of Jewish law undertaken by Maimonides while living in Egypt. Torn between his medical work, his responsibilities as head of the Jewish community, his duties to his family, and his religious studies, between 1170 and 1180 Maimonides still found time and energy to labor on a systematic analysis and ordering of Halakhah, the collective body of Jewish religious laws derived from the Torah and the Talmud, extracting every decision and law therein and arranging them in fourteen rigorously systematic volumes. The Midrash Halakhah, or halakhic exegesis, consists of various rabbinical legal opinions collected throughout the centuries and often quoted in the Talmud to elucidate certain questions. In spite of the traditional Talmudic endorsement, Maimonides believed that the Midrash was not an infallible source for studying and understanding the Law. Midrash was only a methodology, linking the biblical text with the commandments and practical legal precepts by finding associations between both.

The layout of Maimonides' *Mishneh Torah* is guided by a number of systematic principles of interpretation, midrashic and other, taken from older texts, which are not, however, given as sources in the work. Maimonides passes over this in silence, except to say that his original deductions are drawn from the two Talmuds, from the *Sifra* (the halakhic Midrash on Leviticus) and from the Tosefta (a supplement to the Mishnah written mainly in Aramaic).[2] Why Maimonides chose not to reveal the rest of his sources remains an unanswered question.

The search for order is as old as humankind. The arrangement of animal and human figures on the walls of prehistoric caves, the alignment of dolmens, the invention of writing and counting as systems of ordered signs denote a deeply rooted human need for an epistemological grammar to make sense of the scattered offerings presented by an impassive universe. At first this order was sought in religious ritual as an elevated social activity; later (as Simone Weil points out in her criticism of Plato) society began "to imitate the religious up to the point of becoming one with it, barring a supernatural discernment."[3] Under the rule of an emperor or a pope, and later under that of a democratically elected head of government, society became "the only idol," reverting to a state of idol worship like that of pre-Mosaic times, which Maimonides abhorred. Maimonides imagined that a society that recognized and understood the laws that define it would be able to protect itself from idolatry by orderly engagement with the all-embracing deity, not by replacing the recognition of the One with false illusions of star-determined fortune or a multiplicity of pseudonymous images.

For that reason, "the chief object of the Law," Maimonides noted, "is the teaching of truths."[4]

The truth was given to the Jewish people on Mount Sinai. Even though, according to Maimonides, the two essential commandments are the first ones—belief in the existence of a single God and the injunction to forgo idolatry—the Torah lists many more, all discussed in the Talmud, and all meant to assist the Jews in all matters "about which people are perplexed and opinions disagree."[5] Maimonides' ambition was no less than to put the Talmud in order, cautiously following old rabbinical advice: "Teach your tongue to say 'I do not know.'"[6]

The Halakhah, as we know it today, is based on the biblical commandments and the oral Talmudic precepts, as well as customs and traditions compiled in much later books such as the sixteenth-century *Shulchan Aruch*, which drew on the teachings of earlier rabbis. The term "Halakhah" is commonly translated as "Jewish Law," but strictly it denotes "the way to behave or walk," "the way to go about life." The overriding notion in Jewish law is that everything is worthy of attention, even the smallest details of our behavior and that of the world, so that no item is too trivial or inconsequential to study. The Law given by God has to be understood down to its smallest details by means of the power of reason bestowed on us. (This is true also of the laws of Islam. Avicenna, arguing the question of predestination, is of the opinion that human beings "must be bound by one kind of fetter or another—either of the sacred law, or of reason—so that the order of the world may be maintained in full perfection: it is a matter of common observation, that if any man were loosed from both sets of chains the corruption he would commit would be quite intolerable, and the entire order of the world's affairs would be impaired as a result of his relapse from both kinds of fetters.")[7]

This concern with minutiae is essential to understanding the immensity of Maimonides' efforts in ordering and commenting on the 613 laws in his encyclopedic *Mishneh Torah*. Maimonides' aim was to produce an all-inclusive code of law (*sefer kolel*) through which all halakhic material "would be sifted, pruned of associative discussion, digression, and indeterminate debate, and recast in a purified or rarefied form of uniform and normative conclusions and practical directives."[8] His ultimate purpose was to offer a continuity of prescribed behavior which, in turn, would engender an adamant identity to the Jewish people as a whole and to the Jewish individual singly.

Maimonides purposely wrote the work not in Judeo-Arabic but Hebrew because he wanted it to be accessible to every Jewish person, even those beyond the borders of the Arab states, so that "the person who first reads the Written Law and then this compilation, will know from it the whole of the Oral Law, without having occasion to consult another book between them."[9] He gave his work the title *Mishneh Torah* (Repetition of the Torah), but it became known as the *Yad ha-Hazakah* (The Mighty Hand), an allusion to the verse in Deuteronomy, "and in all the mighty hand, and in all the great terror, which Moses wrought in the sight of all Israel."[10] (Maimonides was spoken of as "the Second Moses" and the word *Yad* in Hebrew is written with the same numeric value as the number 14.)

Jorge Luis Borges declared that "the concept of a definitive text belongs either to religion or fatigue."[11] The indefatigable Maimonides spent the remaining years of his life responding to his own rereadings and to the comments of other scholars, revising and correcting sections of his *Mishneh Torah*, creating what can be considered a constantly evolving text and keen on inserting his ongoing emendations in all copies of his book that he could lay his hands on.

Though in many Jewish communities (particularly in Sepharad) the *Mishneh Torah* became almost as popular as the Torah itself and virtually every well-to-do family owned a copy, its first readings received mixed reviews, with a number of critics fiercely opposing it for the absence of sources.[12] Many had the impression that the *Mishneh Torah* was an impious attempt to supersede the direct study of the Talmud, a charge that Maimonides did not deign to answer except to say that he had in his possession what he considered to be several more accurate versions of the Talmud than any of his critics. However, even his most faithful followers understood that in the same way rabbinical scholars thought it impossible to arrive at any conclusion regarding the words of the Mishnah without a knowledge of the discussions and interpretations of the rest of the Talmud, no judgment concerning the *Mishneh Torah* was valid unless other codes were taken into account for the purpose of comparison and reflection. In Jewish thought, only the Torah is incontrovertible. The controversy lay open to all.

The twelfth century was fraught with dissension in the Jewish intellectual and religious world. There was rivalry between the schools that studied the Torah and those that studied the Talmud, and even, among the latter, between those who studied different parts of the Talmud and those who relied on abridged versions of the text. Also there was explicit tension between scholars who concentrated exclusively on the sacred texts and those who spread their nets wider to include science and philosophy. And yet, in spite of the vast array of points of view and fields of interest, the questions that concerned them were essentially the same, and the problems they faced were common to all.

The main opposition to Maimonides' ideas came from the Geonim, the heads of the two great Babylonian Talmudic academies established under the Abbasid caliphate, generally accepted as spiritual leaders of the Jewish community throughout the world. Maimonides, from an essentially Sephardic perspective, judged that the Geonic rulings had local authority only and did not extend over space or time. For example, Maimonides ruled that the Jews of Egypt were allowed to sail on the Sabbath, something the Geonim forbade. To defend his opinion,

Maimonides cited a list of Jewish sages who "before all the Geonim" sailed "the Seville River" (the Guadalquivir of al-Andalus) "all the way to the sea."[13] Tradition tipped the scales on the side of Maimonides' judgment.

Not only were many of the rulings of the Geonim in op-position to Maimonides' opinions. Two centuries before Mai-monides, Saadia Gaon argued that the 613 precepts found in the Torah could be divided into those that were "reasoned" (that is to say, that could be grasped through the rational mind) and those that were "heard" (those given by God to Moses on Sinai that would not have been spontaneously conceived by human intelligence unless God had bestowed them to his people). Mai-monides broke with Gaonic tradition by declaring that all the sacred precepts could be understood by the human mind pro-vided it had intelligence enough. According to Maimonides, the original 613 precepts found in the Torah only had the appear-ance of belonging to different kinds: while some could be un-derstood readily, such as the prohibition on committing murder or stealing, others required learned elucidation but were never beyond the pale of reason. Earlier than the Geonic categories, an old Mosaic tradition divided the 613 precepts into negative (365 "thou shalt nots") and positive (248 "thou shalts"), a divi-sion explicitly laid out in the writings of the third-century Pal-estinian rabbi Simlai, who studied with the grandson of Judah the Prince. These laws were not tabulated until five centuries later, however, when the Gaon Simon Kayyara ordered them in his *Halakot Gedolot*. Reclaiming this venerable tradition, Mai-monides proceeded to classify the 613 precepts into two new main categories: divine commandments and everyday laws. The former belong to the category of the obvious to all; the latter need clarification because they might seem too obscure or even meaningless to persons of lesser understanding. For Maimon-ides, the totality of the precepts in the Torah constitute the basis for monotheistic faith. Anyone who does not recognize

God as the One is deemed an idolater, no matter how fervently the other commandments are followed because, Maimonides ruled, to worship God under a false guise is not to worship him at all. In Maimonides' opinion, the traditional 613 commandments had created confusion among the faithful during the first centuries of Judaism, and in an attempt to remedy this, Maimonides rearranged the commandments in an order that provided the foundation of almost all subsequent classifications. However, allowing himself the eclecticism of a truly intelligent mind, Maimonides frequently deviated from his own system and cited individual commandments which, according to his ordering, could not be considered absolute rules.[14] This philosophical flexibility contained within the legal framework of the *Mishneh Torah* defines Maimonides the thinker.

Several characteristics distinguish Maimonides' *Mishneh Torah* from any other work on Jewish Law, before or after. Showing his extraordinary versatility as a literary writer in both Arabic and Hebrew, and conscious of the importance of this new and ambitious work, Maimonides chose to write his *Mishneh Torah* in a rich, vivid style inspired by the language of the Mishnah: concise, clear, and superbly elegant. He bragged that if he wished, he could have summed up all his writings into a single page.[15] Audaciously departing from the established but seemingly erratic sequences in the Talmud, Maimonides set out a codification that cut through conflicting rabbinical interpretations and learned debates, and presented unequivocal, though mostly undocumented, decisions. Its scope was comprehensive, ignoring what appeared to be contradictions between the theoretical and the practical, and insisting that Halakhah should be studied as a whole, interweaving philosophy, religious law, and civil law in a dazzling display of legal, philological, metaphysical, and scientific knowledge. In writing the *Mishneh Torah* Maimonides succeeded in giving the Jewish people a practical constitution of ethical principles and a model of how to think.

Because of the canonical force of the *Mishneh Torah*, authoritative copies were treasured. One of the most important to have survived is a manuscript of the first two books of the *Mishneh Torah* now in the Bodleian Library that carries the following *nihil obstat:* "It was proofread from my own original book. I am Moses the son of Rabbi Maimon of blessed memory." Several of these manuscripts, together with letters and other documents by Maimonides, were discovered in the Cairo Genizah, a special chamber in the Old Synagogue in which all kinds of papers were preserved to be later properly disposed of in case they carried by chance or purpose the name of God. Inevitably, the Genizah contained material in the hand of Cairo's most celebrated Jewish resident.[16]

As regards Halakhah, no point was considered too trite for explanation, and to achieve this, Maimonides often used common cases drawn from everyday life. An example is his response to the question of whether the components of a Passover meal—lamb, matzoth, and bitter herbs—can be consumed individually if one of the three is missing. The oldest rabbinical texts say that the lamb can be eaten without the matzo or bitter herbs, but that these are valueless without the lamb. Maimonides disagrees with the verdict, saying that these texts offer "only a rabbinical opinion and not a biblical commandment."[17]

Sometimes Maimonides reaches for more uncommon examples. For instance, explaining that according to the law, someone who indirectly enables damage is no less to blame than the person who does damage, Maimonides proposes the following situation: A man who is throwing dishes out of a window places cushions on the ground outside so that the dishes will not break when they fall. Another man comes by and takes the cushions away so that when the first man throws the dishes, they hit the ground and break. In this case, Maimonides decrees, the second man is as liable as the first for damages, in spite of having broken the dishes neither deliberately nor directly: both men were

Cairo Genizah Fragment, written in a Judeo-Arabic dialect,
early thirteenth century, autograph letter of Avraham, son of Maimonides.
(Photo: Historic Collection/Alamy Stock Photo)

responsible for the actions that, combined, caused the break-
age. For the common reader, Maimonides' *Mishneh Torah* is a
sui generis how-to manual.

Other than the *Guide of the Perplexed*, Maimonides' books,
including the *Mishneh Torah*, are seldom read for literary plea-

sure. They are conceived as handbooks to help better understand the Law. Maimonides' intention in choosing a terse, clear style for the *Commentary on the Mishnah* and the *Mishneh Torah* can be explained in the same way Stendhal was to explain his daily reading of the strict Napoleonic Code: "to sound always natural" and "not to charm by false means the reader's soul."[18] Clarity above all was imperative.

In preparation for writing the *Mishneh Torah*, Maimonides had composed the *Sefer HaMitzvot* (Book of Commandments), in which he simply listed all of the 613 precepts, both the positive and the negative. But in the *Mishneh Torah* itself, with a more practical intent in mind, Maimonides divided the precepts into five categories, each based on a degree of obligation. The precepts themselves were then split into fourteen types, each constituting a book. In the first, as a summation of his grand project, Maimonides states his intention of providing the Jewish people with an adequate knowledge of the laws that should guide them toward proper behavior, and in order to provide a context, he discusses a vast variety of subjects, from the nature of God and his angels to the constitution of the cosmos, the gift of revelation, and the systems of rewards and punishments. After this introduction follows the *Mishneh Torah* proper.

The fourteen books of the *Mishneh Torah* are arranged as follows:

Madda (Knowledge)
Ahavah (Love [of God])
Zemanim (Times)
Nashim (Women)
Kedushah (Holiness)
Haflaah (Separation)
Zeraim (Seeds)
Avodah (Divine Service)
Korbanot (Offerings)

Taharah (Ritual Purity)
Nezikim, also known as Nezikin (Torts)
Kinyan (Acquisition)
Mishpatim (Civil Laws)
Shoftim (Judges)

A number of the laws that Maimonides discusses do not seem to have their source in any of the texts he casually mentions. Maimonides might have deduced them himself from personal interpretations of the Torah or from rabbinical writings that have not come down to us. Whatever the case, the *Mishneh Torah* stands as a fundamental text that helps, as Maimonides himself said, to "commence to compose man's mind" guiding us through the laws of the Torah, that "store of great good which the Holy One, blessed is He, hath provided for the social existence of this world, so that the life of the world to come may also be inherited, and be accessible to all, little and great, men and women, to one of broad understanding as well as to one of lesser understanding."[19]

14

The Guide of the Perplexed

Lord, have compassion for wisdom.

—Solomon ibn Gabirol (eleventh century)

SHLOMO PINES, author of the authoritative translation of *The Guide of the Perplexed* into English, points out that "the *Guide* belongs to a very peculiar literary genre, of which it is the unique specimen."[1] Perhaps not unique: Saint Augustine's *City of God* (426), Robert Burton's *Anatomy of Melancholy* (1621), the Prince of Sansevero's *Apologetic Letter* (1751), and Søren Kierkegaard's *Fear and Trembling* (1843) might be said to belong to the same peculiar genre: analytical, rambling, a seemingly all-embracing and illuminating consideration of a difficult and controversial subject: the human capacity for enlightenment.

Lay readers of the Bible who open Maimonides' *Guide* for the first time, perplexed by the many concrete commandments and the host of fantastic tales they have come across in the biblical text, will not find in Maimonides' book the clear instructions and step-by-step clarification they might be hoping for or have come to expect after reading the *Mishneh Torah*. Instead, as Maimonides himself says, the book consists of "dispersed chapters," set down exclusively for the benefit of his disciple Joseph son of Judah and for those like him, "however few they are." These are the worthy "perplexed" (sometimes the translation "irresolute" is preferred; the French choose *égarés*, "lost," the Spanish *perplejos* or *descarriados*, "bewildered" or "led astray"; the Germans *Verwirrten* or *Unschlüssigen*, "confused" or "undecided"; the Italians *perplessi*, "puzzled") for whom the book is intended. Maimonides explains his intentions outright: "It is not the purpose of this Treatise to make its totality understandable to the vulgar or to beginners in speculation, nor to teach those who have not engaged in any study other than the science of the Law. . . . [I]ts purpose is to give indications to a religious man for whom the validity of our Law has become established in his soul and has become actual in his belief."[2] (Maimonides' near contemporary, Avicenna, in his *Mi'raj*, or *Book of the Ladder*, stated a similar caveat: "It is not possible to show the inner meanings of these words to one of the ignorant masses. Only a rationalist is permitted to enjoy the inner meaning of these words.")[3]

Furthermore, the seekers of a full explanation of the sacred books are clearly told that this is not what they will find in the *Guide*. "The first purpose of this Treatise," Maimonides states, "is to explain the meanings of certain terms occurring in books of prophecy." "Certain terms": nothing else. But with the kaleidoscopic eyes to which the reader reluctantly grows accustomed, changing their point of view and the object of their attention at each turn of the page, Maimonides explains that there is indeed a second purpose: "namely, the explanation of very obscure parables [*mashalim*] occurring in the books of the prophets, but not explicitly identified as such." The ignorant may read these only "according to their external meaning." But if Maimonides were to explain the parables and point out that they are indeed parables, these readers might take the right path and be delivered of their confusion. "That is why," Maimonides says, "I have called this Treatise *The Guide of the Perplexed*," because, trapped between philosophical, legal, and religious questions, a person might be haunted by "imaginary beliefs to which he owes his fear and difficulty and would not cease to suffer from heartache and great perplexity."[4] Maimonides proceeded to write the *Guide* in a seemingly rambling, beautifully poetic, deliberately cryptic voice, jumping from point to point and changing the direction of his thoughts midstream, going from strictly logical constructs to metaphysical puzzlements and lucubrations.

The noted historian Shelomo Dov Goitein, reviewing Pines's translation of the *Guide* in 1963, advised the curious reader to begin with the introductions, then go to chapter 32 of part I, which deals with the danger of careless study, "and then to read wherever he is attracted by the subject matter." This seems like excellent advice for explorers of Maimonides' labyrinthine book. If Maimonides deliberately did not render much of the meaning explicit and hid certain revelations behind allusive language, why not allow chance to play a guiding role in the extraordinary maze? "He will be rewarded richly," Goitein concludes.[5] Rather than a proper guide to an intellectual maze, the *Guide* can seem at first glance like an intellectual maze itself.

For instance, if the reader is interested in the subject of prophecy, chapter 32 of the second part of the *Guide* deals with this difficult theme and carries an enticement for the perplexed reader: "When, in the case of a superior individual who is perfect with respect to his rational and moral qualities, his imaginative faculty is in its most perfect state and when he has been prepared in the way that you will hear, he will necessarily become a prophet, inasmuch as this is a perfection that belongs to us by nature. According to this opinion it is not possible that an individual should be fit for prophecy and prepared for it and not become a prophet, except to the extent to which it is pos-

More Newuchim (*Guide for the Perplexed*), Paris, Bibliothèque nationale, Cod. Hebr. 685, Fol. 58. (Photo: akg-images)

sible that an individual having a healthy temperament should be nourished with excellent food, without sound blood and similar things being generated from that food."[6] The false claims of prophecy (and exceptions to the false claims) are one of the subjects of the *Guide*, but there are many more, implicit and explicit.

The question of prophecy is, in part, a question of disposition. If, as Aristotle had argued, the universe owes its existence to fixed and unchangeable laws, such things as miracles and prophecy must be impossible. Prophecy, Maimonides adds to Aristotle's caveat, can be a natural faculty depending on the degree of perfection that a person's other faculties (moral, mental, and physical) might possess. Anyone can become a prophet should the Almighty wish it, but anyone also, depending on the grace of God, might be prevented from flourishing. The perfection of all of God's works sometimes flourishes in his human creatures, some of whom are imbued by a sense of absolute justice (*'adl mahd* in Avicenna's vocabulary), which might allow their reason to attain prophetic wisdom. On one hand, the unchanging and eternal world of God renders the notion of an apocalypse impossible, even when announced in the prophetic voice of an Isaiah. On the other, the prophecies of Moses, received from God himself on Mount Sinai, are valid and true: produced not through angelic intermediaries, and therefore not a fruit of the imagination, but through Moses' own rational faculties. In certain exalted cases, reason allows for prophecy, but even in this case the most important secrets should not be written down, in order to shield them from uninstructed eyes. The medieval scholar Joshua Parens suggests that "perhaps Maimonides did consider it judicious not to draw attention to the role of the imagination in prophecy."[7]

The first part of the *Guide* is largely devoted to these problems, as well as to the metaphorical interpretation of images. What do they mean, the astonishing imagistic stories that appear in the sacred texts? How should we read them and interpret them? What lessons should we draw from the parables to help us on the way to understanding and obedience to the law? Maimonides offers two seemingly contradictory notions of the use of parables in the Bible, and characteristically he presents these opinions as parables. The first compares a *mashal* (a short parable with a moral lesson) to a man who loses a pearl in a dark house, and by means of a cheap candle finds it. For Maimonides, the internal meaning of the words of the Torah is a pearl, while the external meaning of all mashalim is nothing. The second compares the mashalim to an apple of gold in settings of silver (from Proverbs 25:11). When seen from a distance or with distracted attention, it seems that the apple is made of silver, but when someone with keener sight inspects it, that person recognizes that the apple is made of gold. Therefore the external meaning of a mashal, according to Maimonides, has to be as beautiful as silver, while its internal meaning ought to be more beautiful than the external one, as beautiful as gold.

Correlating some of the most powerful of these images— the disobedience in the Garden, the vision of Ezekiel—to a set of essential metaphysical ideas, Maimonides resorts to philological concepts (drawn largely from his Talmudic and Islamic masters) to explain the use of such depictions. In certain cases, the explanation is linguistic: the confusion stems from the use of certain words that are perfect homonyms, referring to two or more different things, or from an imperfect use of words, and these images should be read simply as metaphors.

Maimonides devotes a fair section of the first chapter of part III of his *Guide* to interpreting the prophet Ezekiel's vision of the divine chariot. Ezekiel's vision of the chariot is the first of the prophet's three visions. In it, God approaches Ezekiel in the guise of a divine warrior, driving a battle chariot drawn by four living creatures, each with four wings and four faces: those of a man, a lion, an ox, and an eagle (in which Christian iconography will see the emblems of the Four Evangelists). Next to each of the creatures is a wheel within a wheel with "tall and awesome" rims full of eyes. God orders Ezekiel to become a prophet and stand as a watchman in Israel: "O mortal," says God in Ezekiel's vision, "I am sending you to the people of Israel" (Ezekiel 2:3).

According to the Mishnah, the "Account of the Chariot" may be discussed only orally and with just one other person present, a person with the intellectual capacity to understand this difficult matter according to his or her individual rational powers.[8] Maimonides was aware of these caveats, and also that the times in which he was living were of such an evil nature that the intimate meaning of the sacred text would probably be lost or distorted in the present darkness. This made it all the more important to try to recapture the forgotten explanations by means of his own intellectual powers.

Like the vision of Ezekiel, the question of miracles and miraculous events (did they actually take place? should they be taken literally?) is largely one of language: Maimonides considers that they should be read not as material events but as allegories or metaphors of a deeper truth. For that very reason, their explanations must be elaborately precise. "Your intention," says Maimonides to his readers, "must be not only to understand the totality of the subject of the chapter [in the *Guide*], but also to grasp each word that occurs in it in the course of the speech, even if that word does not belong to the intention of the chapter. For the diction of this Treatise has not been chosen at haphazard, but with great exactness and exceeding precision."[9]

Language is in itself symbolic, a system of signs that carry meaning from the realm of thought and experience to that of communicable expression. Even when expressed "with great exactness and exceeding precision," words are condemned to lose much of their charge in the process. Metaphors are crutches on which language supports itself, and the enlightened reader needs to see those crutches for what they are and recognize the intended communication that they purport to be cumbersomely carrying.

The troubled question of the features of God is also a problem of language. In the same first section of the *Guide*, Maimonides discusses the subject of divine attributes, which, he argues, stem from a misreading of certain passages in the holy text. Here Maimonides applies pure Aristotelian logic to a fundamental question of Jewish faith. An attribute, Aristotle had argued, might denote a quality not inherent in the thing described, in which case it is "an accident"; or, on the contrary, it names a quality that is of the essence in the thing. But if the latter be true, in the case of God a divine attribute would denote a plurality inherent in the Godhead, which cannot, by definition, be the case. God, as Maimonides vehemently explained, simply cannot be defined because a definition can be given only by establishing a particular class of a vaster entity. God is unique and is everything and therefore cannot be divided into parts, either material or spiritual. No comparisons between qualities such as wisdom and sweetness, gentleness and bitterness, strength and weakness found in many creatures can be made between those same creatures and God, since a creature's existence (whatever its qualities) is merely possible, while that of God is absolute. Maimonides repeatedly insists that God is not a concrete being with a tangible form, something or someone existing in a certain moment of time or a certain point in space. Such a being would be a part of the universe, not its overall master. In the Talmud, one of the epithets by which God is referred to is "The Place" because God is the eternal and omnipresent here-and-now of all existence, the ground zero or hypocenter of creation: the universe exists in him, and not he in the universe. The Midrash puts it in these words: "The Holy One, blessed be He, is the place of His universe, but His universe is not His place."[10]

This conception of an immaterial, emotionless, and featureless God did not convince everyone. In the nineteenth century, long after the *Guide* had become a classic of Jewish thought, the same Heinrich Graetz who had praised Maimonides' *Mishneh Torah* as an Ariadne's thread through the halakhic laws scolded Maimonides for this divine abstraction. "Instead of the God of Revelation," Graetz wrote, "who, full of mercy, looks down on humanity, the people of Israel, and every single man," Maimonides posited from the point of view of philosophy "a metaphysical being, which in cold sublimity and seclusion is not allowed to care for its creatures—that its existence should not vaporize in thought."[11] Graetz seems to accuse Maimonides the philosopher of betraying Maimonides the believer.

From about the tenth century, in the Judeo-Arabic tradition, the conflict between philosophy and religion stemmed from the different readings of religion's imagistic language and from the use of logic and reason applied to the miraculous stories and the anthropomorphic depiction of God. Some of the earliest Jewish philosophers, such as Judah ha-Levi and Saadia Gaon, explained these problems away by judging the devices figurative: the supernatural stories in the Bible or the attribution of hands and feet to God should be understood as parabolic or euphemistic.[12] Maimonides went farther and declared that the incorporeality of God was an essential part of Jewish dogma, and that anyone who did not understand and accept this was no less than an idolater. He may have been responding to the perplexity expressed by Galen, in the treatise *On My Own Opinions*, translated prior to the ninth century into Arabic: "Whether the universe is uncreated or created, whether there is something after it or outside it or indeed nothing, because I say that I am in ignorance faced with such questions, I also do not know of course what is the nature of the creator of all things in the universe, if he is incorporeal or corporeal, and more, in what place he resides."[13] To that question Maimonides had a straightforward answer.

Maimonides did not, however, have a straightforward answer regarding the doctrine of resurrection. Some readers of his *Guide* deduced from certain passages in the book that resurrection was not an indisputable promise, this in spite of Maimonides' assertion in the thirteenth and last of his *Principles:* "I believe with perfect faith that the dead will be brought back to life when God wills it to happen."[14] The controversy became so heated that the head of the Talmudic Academy of Baghdad, Samuel ben Ali, accused Maimonides of heresy for denying this basic tenet that Maimonides himself had previously endorsed. Thirteen years before his death, from his overworked position in Fustat, Maimonides responded with *Essay on Resurrection*, acknowledging the ambiguity inherent in his *Guide*. "It is not rare," he wrote, "that a person aims to expound the intent of some conclusions clearly and explicitly, makes an effort to reject doubts and eliminate far-fetched interpretations, and yet the unbalanced will draw the reverse judgment of the conclusion he sought to clarify." People of little understanding concentrate on narrative details for the most part allegorical, such as (in the case of resurrection) "asking if the dead will rise naked or in their garments, and other such problems. But the world-to-come is entirely overlooked."[15] The world to come is, for Maimonides, the time and place where the Jewish people will attain understanding and wisdom for which they must strive now: the achievement, for those intellectually gifted, of a state of spiritual bliss through perseverant study.

Maimonides distinguished between the Messianic Era (*yemot ha-mashiach*, literally, "the days of the Messiah") and the Afterlife (*olam ha-ba*, "the world to come"). Maimonides could therefore, honestly and forcefully, declare his belief that form and body can be restored, will in fact be restored, in the Messianic Era, and that ultimately bodily form, which decays, will disappear at the end of historical time. The soul, however, which is eternal (in created time), will ultimately become disembodied in the Afterlife, where it will enjoy eternal bliss.

Maimonides goes on to say that "the Resurrection is a fundamental of the Torah of Moses our master."[16] However, the Jewish Bible does not discuss the question except in four instances, Isaiah 26:19, Daniel 12:2, Psalms 71:20 and Ezekiel 37:13–14. (Ezekiel in particular seems clearly to prophesy a general resurrection: "You shall know, O My people, that I am the LORD, when I have opened your graves and lifted you out of your graves. I will put My breath into you and you shall live again." In spite of the fact that none of these sites deals with the matter of resurrection in any depth, by the twelfth century belief in the resurrection became an undisputed doctrine in Judaism. In Islam as well, resurrection is a tenet of faith, since it is mentioned specifically in the Qur'an. But for the philosophically minded in both Jewish and Islamic thought, resurrection presented insurmountable logical problems, and Maimonides (like Averroës in Islam) chose not to address them directly. Maimonides postponed the debate, saying that resurrection would take place but not until the coming of the Messiah, thus relegating the question to the end of time. His discussion of the problem in *Essay on Resurrection* is at best a circumvention. "The masses," he writes, "do not recognize existence except of a body or what is in a body. . . . What I do deny and disown before God is any assertion that the soul will never return to the body, and that it simply cannot happen."[17] In the *Commentary on the Mishnah*, Maimonides insists on the impossibility of understanding this by those who limit their knowledge to the bodily realm: "Know that just as the blind man cannot imagine color, as the deaf person cannot experience sounds, and as the eunuch cannot feel sexual desire, so bodies cannot attain spiritual delights. Like fish, who do not know what the element of fire is, because they live upon its opposite, the element of water, so are the delights of the spiritual world unknown in this material world."[18] Maimonides believed that for someone philosophically enlightened (such as himself) it was possible to harmonize belief in a resurrection postponed with the knowledge of "spiritual delights" and the corruptible nature of everything human.[19]

But not every fantastic tale in the Bible is to be considered fictional. Regarding the accounts of certain miracles such as the story of creation in the book of Genesis, Maimonides argued that they accorded with Aristotle's teachings: any objections to their verisimilitude can be dismissed (once again) as misreadings. Adam's transgression is for Maimonides a complex metaphor concerning the relationship between the intellectual, sensation, and moral faculties, in the same way that the three sons of Adam are set up as allegories of the vegetable, the animal, and the intellectual components of a human being. Underlying these affirmations, readers sense that what Maimonides is asking them to do is to translate into literal discourse the ancient fabulous tales. But then he veers off again: "Some are valid truths, and some are undoubtedly fables; others raise the question: are they fact or fiction? If you study in depth everything written by the sages and by the Andalusian commentators, and the context of the doubtful passage, it will become clear to you."[20]

Aristotle, rejecting the notion of the truth of myths, nevertheless admitted that the wonder produced by miraculous stories could be of use to the inquiring mind, as long as they are treated not as straightforward truths but as allegories leading to the truth. In the *Metaphysics*, he writes, "It is through wonder that men now begin and originally began to philosophize; wondering in the first place at obvious perplexities, and then by gradual progression raising questions about the greater matters too, *e.g.* about the changes of the moon and of the sun, about the stars and about the origin of the universe. Now he who wonders and is perplexed feels that he is ignorant (thus the myth-lover is in a sense a philosopher, since myths are composed of wonders); therefore if it was to escape ignorance that men studied philosophy, it is obvious that they pursued science for the sake of knowledge, and not for any practical utility."[21]

To those who wonder and remain perplexed, the question of allegory is problematic, but at the same time of the essence, since no sacred text avoids allegories. Centuries later, in 1818, commenting on the idea of allegory from the point of view of a European Romantic, Coleridge, who had read Maimonides and admired him, argued that monotheistic religion had brought on an opposition "to the spirit of pagan Greece, which receiving the very names of its gods from Egypt, soon deprived them of all that was universal. The Greeks changed the ideas into finites, and these finites into *anthropomorphi*, or forms of men." Coleridge, adopting Maimonides' allegorical explanation for the serpent's role in the fall, echoed his question: If Adam and Eve sinned, how could they be rewarded with knowledge?[22]

"Knowledge," Coleridge wrote in a Maimonidean vein, "in Hebraic thought, is not 'forbidden'; it is the highest good, the reward of all efforts. The explanation lies in the qualification of that knowledge: it is the 'knowledge of good and evil,' which is a descent from total perception of truth to a fragmentation and division, a dualism within the self, whereby moralism and convention replace the clarity of a once-unified wholeness of outer and inner vision."[23] For Coleridge as a Romantic, the reverse of this was the natural effect "in which finites, even the human form, must, in order to satisfy the mind, be brought into connexion with, and be in fact symbolical of, the infinite; and must be considered in some enduring, however shadowy and indistinct, point of view, as the vehicle or representative of moral truth."[24] Hence the use of allegorical language.

Like Coleridge long after him, Maimonides believed in a universal mind and in the common source of the essential questions. Whether through philosophical or religious readings, whether in straightforward precepts or by means of fables, the teachings of the Torah, Maimonides argued, can be called Jewish only because the Jews were the first to discover them. From an ethnical standpoint, Maimonides believed, these teachings are no more Jewish than the elements of Euclid are Greek. Embedded as he was in the Mediterranean culture of the twelfth century, Maimonides shared throughout his life a rich variety of cultural experiences in the several countries to which his forced wanderings took him. By "Mediterranean" we should not understand a closely knit cultural identity.[25] On the contrary. Maimonides, as already said, identified himself with the specific culture of Sepharad in which he was born. He signed his name Moshe ben Maimon ha-Sepharadi ("the Spaniard") and even later, as an exile in North Africa, Palestine, and Egypt, he continued to assert his ties to his Sephardic ancestors. However, Maimonides recognized that other cultures expressed precious considerations that could not be dismissed. For Maimonides the rational mind had to find ways of incorporating these into the Law, in spite of ages-old opposition. "No man should believe anything," Maimonides strenuously affirmed, "unless attested by one of three principles. First, rational proof as in mathematical sciences; secondly, the perception by one of the five senses . . . and thirdly, tradition as derived from the prophets and the righteous."[26] In statements like this, Maimonides stands as the emblematic believer in rationality as the single most powerful instrument for approaching the truth. Coleridge, once more, echoed this Maimonidean belief in 1818: "This again is the mystery and the dignity of our human nature, that we cannot give up our reason, without giving up at the same time our individual personality. . . . He who asserts that truth is of no importance except in the sense of sincerity, confounds sense with madness, and the word of God with a dream."[27]

And yet, because human intelligence is limited, to be allowed a glimpse of what lies in the mysterious realm beyond reason, contemplation of the universe is the ultimate way for the true seeker. Maimonides instructs his readers to look upon the beauty of things, whether the sphere of stars adored by the people of Abraham or the walls of your room "while you lie awake upon your bed," or gaze upon the quiet flowers of a garden reminiscent of those of Córdoba.[28] In these moments of reverential gaze, deepening one's awe and appreciation for the Creator through his creation, something might be sparked of the light that shone in Eden.

Maimonides illustrates this with an allegorical parable in part III of the *Guide*, of a king in a secluded palace and of the people who wish to reach him, some inside the city and some outside. For the modern reader, Maimonides' parable has something Kafkaesque about it, because it entails a long and laborious journey that never (or hardly ever) reaches its prescribed destination, however much it seems to be within the traveler's reach. To come unto the king one has to traverse seven levels. The first contains the people who have no knowledge of the Law and are therefore barely human. The second belongs to those who are looking in the wrong direction and, consciously or not, have turned their backs on the king. In the third are those who have entered the palace and believe they observe the Law but nevertheless remain ignorant of the truth of the commandments. The fourth has those who have legal knowledge of the commandments but not of the foundations of the faith. The fifth is the level of those who have succeeded in entering but remain wandering in the antechambers arguing about the tenets of religion. The sixth belongs to those who have come at last into the presence of the king because they have studied deeply and, as far as their intelligence permits, have found answers to great questions, but have not yet seen the king or spoken with him. Finally, in the seventh are those who have successfully come upon the king and, with an effort beyond their human intelligence, may, if he is willing, be granted the privilege of speaking with him and hearing him speak.[29] Until reaching that last stage, reason must prevail.

Even certain basic tenets of Judaism, such as the messianic idea which Maimonides takes as an article of faith (he includes it in twelfth place among the *Thirteen Principles*)[30] can be embraced in tandem with severe anti-apocalyptic caveats. Maimonides does not deny the events outright, catastrophic and otherwise, announced in the prophecies that flourished before and during his time, but he relegates them to the field of the unknowable, to be revealed only when the time of these events comes to pass, and unable to be anticipated by the human mind. One can confirm that something will happen only if and when it happens: prophecy can be called true only after it has been fulfilled. To go back to the question of prophecy—this, for Maimonides, is the essential difference between divine prophecy and superstitious divination: the one is willed by God, the other is born to a credulous mind.[31]

However, Maimonides did not believe in a cause-and-effect relationship between the coming of the Messiah and present human behavior. Men and women must be capable of complying with the Law and fashioning their future by themselves, as Plato argued in book 4 of *The Republic* and as Saint Augustine also embraced (with caveats), translating this idea into the Christian terms of free will. For Maimonides, we choose whether or not to follow the Law at our peril. "Now this can come about only after the adoption of intellectual beliefs," he wrote in the Introduction to part I of the *Guide*, "the first of which being His apprehension, may He be exalted, according to our capacity. This, in its turn, cannot come about except through divine science, and this divine science cannot become actual except after a study of natural science. This is so since natural science borders on divine science, and its study precedes that of divine science in time as has been made clear to whoever has engaged in speculation on these matters."[32] For Maimonides, all laws (including the Law of God) must have two ideals: social well-being and the development of the intellect. Both will be strengthened with the coming of the Messiah, but they will not be initiated by his presence. We all, in our own time, hold the keys to these ideals.

"In that which has occurred to me with regard to these matters," Maimonides explains with simple honesty, "I followed conjecture and supposition; no divine revelation has come to me to teach me that the intention in the matter in question was such and such, nor did I receive what I believe in these matters from a teacher." For as he also acknowledges, "If I had omitted setting down something of that which has appeared to me as clear, so that that knowledge would perish when I perish, as is inevitable, I should have considered that conduct as extremely cowardly with regard to you and everyone who is perplexed."[33] Maimonides was forty-two years old at the time; his *Guide of the Perplexed* was to mark the summit of Jewish medieval thought, a true yet perplexing guide for those whose intellectual curiosity permitted them to conceive the questions that might lead to an understanding and to a higher degree of knowledge. The first of these perplexed readers, as we can see, was Maimonides himself.

Yet, as Maimonides argued, there is an important distinction between what one is permitted to know and the secret things that must remain outside our ken. One of the several explanations given in the exegetic literature as to why the Torah begins not with the first letter of the Hebrew alphabet, *aleph*, but with the second, *bet*, is that the answer appears symbolically in bet's shape. "As the letter *bet* is closed on all sides and only open in front," wrote the second century BCE Hellenistic scholar Ben Sira, "you are to regard as closed to inquiry what was before creation or what is behind; what is open begins from the actual time of creation."[34] Faced with the bewildering nature of a world in a state of constant change that seems to preclude deep, clear, and detailed exploration, which are then the areas open to human inquiry? The question that Michel de Montaigne would adopt as his motto in the sixteenth century, *Que sais-je?* (What do I know?), is, in Jewish thought, necessarily preceded by "What can I know?" and "How can I know it?" This, in turn, brings up the practical, all-essential question: "How should I live?"

The *Guide* offers three possible paths to enlightenment. The first, the path of faith, of reflection upon the One who is beyond words, of illumination through ineffable vision. The second, the study of the Law and the pursuit of lawful behavior both in private and in public, as a member of the communal fold. The third, a life dedicated to good governance, following God in the world, engaged in the life of the polis (the political life of the community) as a reformer or a teacher or a leader. Maimonides does not make the choice for us. But all three require ethical conduct and a truthful mind.

The Introduction to the *Guide* includes an entreaty from Maimonides not to share with others the knowledge that the *Guide* will reveal to the intended reader, removing "a screen from between the eye and a visible thing." He quotes the Babylonian Talmud: "*The Account of the Beginning ought not to be taught in the presence of two men*" and extrapolates that if someone were to explain all those matters in a book, "he in effect would be *teaching* them to thousands of men."[35] This is one the essential paradoxes of the *Guide:* restricted illumination.

"No historian who has a sense of decency and therefore a sense of respect for a superior man such as Maimonides," wrote Leo Strauss, "will disregard light-heartedly the latter's emphatic entreaty not to explain the secret teaching of the *Guide*. It may fairly be said that an interpreter who does not feel pangs of conscience when attempting to explain that secret teaching and perhaps when perceiving for the first time its existence and bearing lacks that closeness to the subject which is indispensable for the true understanding of any book. Thus the question of adequate interpretation of the *Guide* is primarily a moral one."[36] Or perhaps it is a question of the fitness of the student, as if Maimonides (to put this in a modern academic context) were not willing to admit first-year students into a graduate seminar for fear they would be overwhelmed and distraught by not understanding. And as the leader of the Jewish community of his time, he knew the stakes were infinitely greater.

Maimonides' advice on personal ethics—how to behave toward oneself and toward one's fellow creatures—stems both from his life experience and from his vast reading. Maimonides lists among these the obvious obligations of keeping one's body healthy and clean, of seeking medical advice in case of sickness, and of honestly earning one's daily bread; spiritually, to seek contentment for the soul and to find a middle ground between ecstasy and grief, not expecting the permanence of either.

As to our social behavior, Maimonides, following Jewish tradition, refers to King Solomon as the emblematic example of a wise man deceived into believing that by virtue of his privileged intellect he had been able to transcend 3 of the 613 precepts (the ones commanding the proper behavior of a king) while observing the commandments themselves.[37] The book of Kings tells that God appeared to King Solomon during the night in a dream, and said, "Ask, what shall I grant you?" Solomon answered:

> You dealt most graciously with Your servant my father David, because he walked before You in faithfulness and righteousness and in integrity of heart. You have continued this great kindness to him by giving him a son to occupy his throne, as is now the case. And now, O LORD my God, You have made Your servant king in place of my father David; but I am a young lad, with no experience in leadership. Your servant finds himself in the midst of the people You have chosen, a people too numerous to be numbered or counted. Grant, then, Your servant an understanding mind to judge Your peo-

ple, to distinguish between good and bad; for who can judge
this vast people of Yours?"

God was pleased that Solomon had asked for this and said to
him:

> Because you asked for this—you did not ask for long life, you
> did not ask for riches, you did not ask for the life of your en-
> emies, but you asked for discernment in dispensing justice—I
> now do as you have spoken. I grant you a wise and discerning
> mind; there has never been anyone like you before, nor will
> anyone like you arise again. And I also grant you what you
> did not ask for—both riches and glory all your life—the like
> of which no king has ever had. And I will further grant you
> long life, if you will walk in My ways and observe My laws and
> commandments, as did your father David. (1 Kings 3:4–14)

Whether for Solomon or for the common man, Maimonides maintained, the 613 precepts must be held as sacred, and in
our behavior toward others, whether free or slaves, we should
practice the essential qualities of charity and amiability, together with a knowledge of and respect for justice, dealing as
honorably as we can with our fellow human beings.

15

What Is Virtue?

If, then, the virtues are neither passions nor
faculties, all that remains is that they
should be states of character.

—Aristotle, *Nicomachean Ethics*, 2.5

BOTH THE *Epistle to Yemen* and the *Epistle on Conversion* are
concerned with the problem of how to deal with contemporary
catastrophes without increasing the anguished state of individ-
uals and that of the whole community, while at the same time
underlining the importance of adhering tenaciously to the Jewish faith and the Law. In the address to Rabbi Ya'akov, Maimonides put forward an argument concerning the proper conduct
of a Jew, and then proceeded to develop in depth the question
What constitutes virtue?

For Aristotle, virtue lies in the imitation of nature, but since
this is an ideal, social laws and rational judgment are necessary
to guide us toward it. For Maimonides however, virtue lies not
in the imitation of nature but in the will of the unknowable
God. Certainly, nature has to be studied. To his student Joseph

ben Judah, whom Maimonides addresses in his Epistle Dedicatory of the *Guide*, he says repeatedly that his studies require a gradual order: first logic, second mathematics, then natural sciences, and finally metaphysics. One of Joseph's main errors has been to ignore the natural sciences and plunge straight into metaphysical questions. The study of nature is essential to achieving enlightenment.[1]

However, according to Maimonides, the virtuous human qualities belong either to the appetitive faculty or to the deliberative faculty; they can consequently be divided into moral and intellectual virtues or vices. Courage (moral) and reflection (intellectual) are virtues deriving from these different faculties, for instance, just as cowardly and rash actions would be vices corresponding to the same division. Maimonides provides a number of useful definitions, scattered throughout his writings. Virtue is an action of the will to do what is approved by reason, and it stems from a natural potential for action. Virtue, in order to grow and expand, requires exercise and intelligence. Ethical virtue is the permanent direction of the will which maintains our best conduct, and it is intellectually determined. A virtuous life (as previously noted) should not depend on the coming of the Messiah. We should await it hopefully, of course, but not weigh our actions according to the promised expectation.[2]

Virtue requires courage, the middle point between cowardice and rash audacity, the spiritual temperance that lies between unrestrained desire and stolid indifference. Concerning measured courage, Maimonides refers to an episode in the Tanakh in which a priest addresses the people on the eve of battle, exhorting them to have courage and not fear the enemy. Maimonides understood this verse as normative. Both in the *Mishneh* and the *Sefer HaMitzvot* he lists as a negative prohibition the opposite of cowardice: not having fear of the enemy.[3] The Talmud gives the following example. In the second century BCE, a slave of King Yannai of Judea killed a man, and the king him-

Mishneh Torah, Fol. 40v, Perugia, Italy, fourteenth century (text), ca. 1400 (illumination), showing a priest giving a blessing, from the collection of the National Library of Israel. (Photograph from the Ursula and Kurt Schubert Archives at the Center for Jewish Art, The Hebrew University of Jerusalem)

self was called to account for this action by the rabbinical court. When Shimon ben Shetah, a Pharisee scholar and rabbinical judge, asked the king to stand, Yannai replied, "I will do not what you say but what your colleagues say." When Shimon looked right and left, he saw that his fellow judges had their eyes cast on the ground. This, according to the Talmud, is an example of the king's courage in contrast with the cowardly behavior of the judges.[4]

Can virtue be taught? The dialogue *Protagoras* was not among the works of Plato translated into Arabic before Maimonides' time, but the ideas about virtue therein contained surfaced in a number of other Greek texts that would have been accessible to Maimonides in Arabic translation.[5] The dialogue opposes the views of Socrates to those of the philosopher Protagoras, who maintains that virtue can be taught (he accepted payment for teaching it) based on a pattern of empathetic social behavior found, in varying degrees, among all citizens. Socrates is of the opinion that virtue is equal to a degree of knowledge that allows one to differentiate between what is good and what is evil in the same way that one differentiates between pleasure and pain, and he argues that this virtue, alas, is available to only a few.[6] Maimonides' explicit intention of not making his *Guide* "totally understandable to the vulgar" shares the Socratic view of hierarchies of intelligence. Some may be led to enlightenment and are therefore gifted with the virtue of inherent courage; others, the Divine Will has decreed, are not. If Maimonides had imagined an ideal utopia for the Jewish people it might have been inspired by that of Al-Farabi, whom Maimonides considered an authority only below Aristotle, who imagined a government whose perfect sovereign ruled without written laws and altered the norms of conduct of his subjects in accordance with the changes of the time, as he judged proper.[7] Or it might have resembled that of Plato, governed by a philosopher king, a ruler possessed of love for wisdom and the intelligence to attain that wisdom for the individual and public good.[8] A wise ruler will therefore prescribe moral habits that must be repeated until they become part of society's character. "If a man will always carefully discriminate as regards his actions, directing them to the medium course, he will reach the highest degree of perfection possible to a human being, thereby approaching God and sharing in His happiness."[9]

In the last two paragraphs of his *Mishneh Torah*, Maimonides describes the coming of the Messiah in these words: "The Messiah will arise and restore the kingdom of David to its former might. He will rebuild the sanctuary and gather the dispersed of Israel. All the laws will be reinstituted in his days as of old. Sacrifices will be offered and the Sabbatical and Jubilee years will be observed exactly in accordance with the commandments in the Torah. But whoever does not believe in him or does not await his coming denies not only the rest of the prophets, but also the Torah and our teacher Moses." Maimonides sternly adds, "Do not think that the Messiah needs to perform signs and miracles, bring about a new state of things in the world, revive the dead, and the like. It is not so. . . . The whole world would be occupied solely with the knowledge of God."[10] Maimonides imagines Paradise as a holistic academy, an end-of-history Eden of intellectual bliss.

The date of this promised coming cannot be known and should not matter to one who wishes to lead a virtuous life. The Jews will survive only if they strictly follow the Law of God given to them through Moses, because "by its teaching, the Heavenly Legislator intended to constitute us an entirely distinct people." And yet, Maimonides continues to say, this choice was not due to the Jews' inherent worth (a fact however distinctly stated in the Scriptures) "but because our progenitors acted righteously through their knowledge of the Supreme Being." It is thanks to the behavior of the virtuous elders that their descendants now "reap the benefit of their meritorious deeds."[11] Here the reader senses a contradiction between fatefully benefiting from the good behavior of our elders and "the elected scholarly inheritance that overrides that of one's own flesh and blood" mentioned earlier. But perhaps both inheritances are liable to coexist.

Gershom Scholem noted that under Maimonides the messianic idea took on a rationalistic quality that it did not have previously. According to Scholem, with Maimonides, "the utopian element quite peculiarly recedes and is only maintained at a bare minimum." The supreme good promised with the advent of the Messiah will consist of a full "contemplative life which the medieval philosophers, on account of the presuppositions of their Greek philosophical legacy, were bound to regard as the ideal of a fulfilled life." Only through the study of the Torah, "that highest realm of contemplation," wrote Maimonides, can the world of Jewish thought with its many laws and obligations be properly illuminated, and through it virtue attained. Maimonides never doubted the superior worth of such an illuminating path. Scholem concludes his reading of Maimonides' virtuous ideal in the *Guide* with these dismissive words: "It is possible to develop this idea of a contemplative life without any reference to the Messianic idea."[12]

The twelfth of Maimonides' *Thirteen Principles of Faith* reads, "I believe with perfect faith in the coming of the Messiah. How long it takes, I will await his coming every day." But this promise lies in the indiscernible future. Here and now, men and women have to strive to see that the gates of wisdom are opened. And when they are, "and these places are entered into, the souls will find rest therein, the eyes will be delighted, and the bodies will be eased of their toil and of their labour."[13]

16

Reading Maimonides

You [Maimonides] have gained fame through the
treasure of your learning everywhere.

—Jonathan ben David ha-Kohen mi-Lunil
(1135–1205), *Commentary on the Mishnah*

A man shall be commended according to his wisdom.

—Proverbs 12:8

No writer can foresee, control, or, even less, determine
the reactions of his or her audience. The writer exits the stage
as soon as the last full stop has been dotted on the page. After
that, the fate of the text is in the hands of its readers, and in their
judgment. Authors cannot bring to bear accusations of unfair-
ness or incorrectness, nor can they take responsibility for whatever interpretation the readers put on their words. They cannot
whisper to the reader, like the Gnat in *Through the Looking-Glass:*
"You might make a joke on that."[1] The reader is the absolute
authority.

Maimonides' two masterworks, the *Mishneh Torah* and *The Guide of the Perplexed,* escaped almost immediately the scope of the author's stated intentions. Maimonides had explained that in writing the *Mishneh Torah,* he had merely wanted to provide a concise and clear instrument that would help the student of the Talmud wind his way through the mazes of the lengthy, convoluted, and essential text. He acknowledged that he had worked on the texts of the Talmud idiosyncratically, omitting certain opinions that he deemed contrary to his own views, such as the superstitious beliefs in charms, portents, and otherworldly demons, and in the field of medical science, for instance, he ignored Talmudic injunctions against things supposedly injurious to a person's health because as a doctor he knew them through experience to be harmless.

If the *Mishneh Torah* was meant as a reorganized vade mecum to the Law, the *Guide* was imagined as a conceptual chart that Maimonides wished to offer certain intelligent but puzzled students of Scripture to shed a helping light on their search; both his admirers and his foes turned the books into adamant monuments that stood imposingly on their own and demanded dogmatic reading. Maimonides himself had severely declared in the *Guide:* "I adjure—by God, may He be exalted!—every reader of this Treatise of mine not to comment upon a single word of it and not to explain to another anything in it save that which has been explained and commented upon in the words of the famous Sages of our Law who preceded me."[2] In this, the Rambam was superbly disobeyed.

In spite of Maimonides' injunction, his writings seemed to invite, even demand, questions from the audience, and thus quickly they became the object of exegesis and criticism. The *Mishneh Torah,* for example, produced whole libraries of commentaries, many more than other halakhic codes. Some of his admirers took his word so strictly that they insisted that a rabbinical tribunal could not issue a judgment contrary to Maimonides' views, even when these views seemed to go against the sense of a Talmudic passage. The famous eighteenth-century Talmudist Malachi ben Jacob ha-Kohen argued that in such cases, it should be deemed that the ancient rabbis had not interpreted the Talmud correctly. Such absolutist readings, however, went clearly against Maimonides' stated intentions. It is true that Maimonides had argued that in the case of conflict between the reading of a biblical text and reason, reason must prevail: reason must be the overriding instrument for understanding not only the word of the Torah (that is to say, the Law) but even the concept of God himself. This led Talmudic students to engage in what was called in Yiddish *Erleydigen a Shveren Rambam* (resolving a difficult Maimonides [passage]).[3]

Maimonides believed that there would always be further discoveries in the sacred texts, made through the eyes of other "reasonable" readers like himself, and that the ongoing study of the Talmud and its commentaries was an essential part of Jewish intellectual life. Truly faithful Jews should not limit themselves to any particular source outside the Torah: Maimonides himself had lectured, for example, on the twelfth-century Talmudist Isaac Alfasi's *Sefer ha-Halachot* (Book of Jewish Legal Matters) drawn from the Babylonian Talmud, to which Maimonides compared his own projected Halachot based on the Palestinian one.[4] Maimonides understood that a searcher for the truth needed to be as widely read as possible.

But a number of anti-rationalist conservative Jews, unable to reconcile the different aspects of the man who was at the same time a learned scientist, a brilliant philosopher, and a keen religious devotee, branded Maimonides a *min*, heretic, and shunned his writings. Not only were Maimonides' philosophical ideas rejected; many of his legal opinions too were judged unacceptable by the traditionalists. For example, Maimonides had argued that the Geonim who ruled over many of the exiled communities, and who profited from their position through

stipends and donations, should earn their living with other oc-
cupations; this was not seen by those concerned with sympathetic eyes. Long after Maimonides' death, debate over pronouncements like these sparked fierce quarrels that lasted for
decades.

In 1305, the Talmudist Solomon ben Abraham Adret of Bar-
celona issued a *herem* (ban) against all allegorical readings inspired by the writings of Maimonides: "Those who say about
Abraham and Sarah that in reality they symbolize matter and
form; that the 12 tribes of Israel are [an allegory] for the 12 plan-
ets, . . . that the Urim and Thummim are to be understood as
the astrolabe instrument . . . [s]ome of them say that everything
in the Torah, from *Bereshit* to the giving of the law, is entirely
allegorical." "Those," it was understood, meant above all the
Rambam himself. Maimonides' son Avraham was outraged:
these scholars, he chided, "are mistaken. They cling to the lit-
eralistic sense of biblical verses, Midrashim, and *aggadot*. This
pains our heart. . . . How could such an impurity, so like the
impurity of idol worship, come to be in Israel?"[5] Several Kab-
balists, notably Meir ibn Gabbai, exiled from his native Spain,
went as far as blaming Maimonides and his writings for the
misfortunes that befell the Sephardic Jews in the fourteenth
and fifteenth centuries.[6] Others translated into their rejection
of Maimonides their personal resentment toward the Christian
and Muslim world, seeing in the Rambam's philosophical explo-
rations an opening that weakened the tenets of true Judaism,
thereby allowing the Gentile authorities to exert power over
them.

Shortly after Maimonides' death, a compromise was reached:
it was decided that no one should study Maimonides before the
age of twenty-five. And yet, as with most intellectual interdic-
tions and censorships throughout the centuries and in all cultures, the anti-rationalist bans were not very effective. On the
contrary, in many cases, these reactions spurred the curious

spirits to seek out the controversial texts and see for themselves what tremendous pronouncements they might contain. When, toward the end of the thirteenth century, the French Talmudist Shlomo Petit traveled to Italy to gather support for his anti-Maimonidean campaign, he was forced to leave the country empty-handed.[7] However, the accusation that Maimonides' reading of the Law adulterated the basic tenets of Judaism and dangerously allowed the Word of God to be contaminated by foreign (i.e., Greek) thought did not altogether disappear. In the nineteenth century, the notable biblical scholar Shmuel David Luzzatto declared that Maimonides was "a great causer of distress to us" because he had transformed the laws of Halakhah from good and useful guides for the people to "implanted nails which do not move from their place."[8]

If the *Mishneh Torah* provoked both outrage and devotion among its readers in search of legal practical enlightenment, *The Guide of the Perplexed* elicited even stronger reactions. As late as the eighteenth century, the German Talmudist Jacob Emden, known as Ya'avetz, judging that the pious rabbi who had composed the *Mishneh Torah* could not possibly have penned the *Guide*, concluded that it was the work of a heretic and con-man, and that the treatise had been falsely attributed to the great Rambam.[9] And the celebrated rabbi Nachman of Bratslav, great-grandson of the Baal Shem Tov, the founder of Hasidism, thunderingly declared, "Whosoever wishes to guard himself [from evil] must distance himself as much as possible from the analytical writings [such as] the *Guide of the Perplexed* of the Rambam."[10]

And yet the *Guide* was to have a long and fruitful afterlife. Soon after it was translated into Hebrew by Samuel ibn Tibbon, scholars throughout the Jewish world read, studied, and discussed it in yeshivas and academies, producing a vast body of varied critical commentaries, based mainly on Ibn Tibbon's translation, with a few inspired directly by Maimonides' original

Judeo-Arabic text. Ibn Tibbon had judged that his translation should suffice. "Everything I interpret in the way of wisdom," he wrote, "I interpret only according to what Maimonides' opinion would be in these things, in accordance with what is revealed in his books." And quoting the Haggadah, he added, "I drink from his water and make others drink."[11] Ibn Tibbon's chutzpah paid off. For centuries, his translation was considered the standard text.

The readers who praised the *Guide* unwaveringly saw in it a salutary scripture, one that prepared the way of the soul toward what Aristotle had called eudaemonia, the highest human good, which is achieved through "the active exercise of the soul's faculties in conformity with rational principle."[12] For several centuries following Ibn Tibbon's translation, a flood of interpretations and exegeses appeared couched in many different styles and genres, not only traditional prose commentaries but also poems praising the *Guide*, biblical-style commentaries that followed the methods set forth by the Rambam, weekly sermons that dwelt on particular passages, letters between scholars pondering difficult points. As study aids for this vast enterprise, writers produced Maimonidean dictionaries and glossaries, condensations and indexes, guides to the *Guide* and introductions. "In terms of literary diversity," wrote one historian, "the *Guide* has engendered a library vaster than that of any other text of Jewish philosophy."[13]

The first full commentary made of the *Guide* was left unfinished in 1279 upon the death of its author, Moses ben Solomon de Salerno. Of his life little is known, except that he must have lived in either Naples or Sicily since he was employed as a Jewish scholar in the court of Frederick II, the enlightened emperor known as *Stupor mundi*, "Wonder of the World." Frederick maintained a friendly relationship with both the Muslim and the Jewish communities; however, because he seems to have denied the concept of the soul's immortality, Dante placed him in his *Inferno* in the circle of the Epicureans. At Frederick's court, Moses de Salerno became engaged in various Jewish-Christian polemics popular at the time. In a work titled *Ta'anot* (Objections) he employed philosophical arguments drawn from Maimonides' *Guide* to refute a number of points in the Christian dogma. Only his commentaries of parts I and II of the *Guide* have reached us, without a preface or introduction, which is odd for a Jewish commentary of the time. It is possible that the text as it now stands, presented as a triangular exchange between Maimonides himself, Moses de Salerno, and a perhaps apocryphal Christian scholar, and consisting of many paraphrases, literal quotations, and explanations set out in dialogue form, was intended merely as a scholastic exercise to be copied out by students and used to study the *Guide* in lieu of Maimonides' original.

Two unusual aspects define Moses de Salerno's commentary. One is the justification for merely quoting or paraphrasing Maimonides rather than offering an in-depth reading intended to illuminate the passage in question. In this Moses de Salerno respected Maimonides' wish to allow certain sections of the *Guide* to remain obscure, especially the mashalim, the biblical parables referred to in the text. In support of his decision, Moses de Salerno quotes Ibn Tibbon on the fact that oral communication is far superior to the written word, an instrument deemed unsuitable for pedagogical endeavors since teaching should be done face to face, through oral examples. When writing, Ibn Tibbon argued, especially when using metaphors and parables, the author needs to proceed with infinite esoteric caution in order not to reveal unwittingly things that should remain secret. This paradoxically seems to undermine the very text that puts the argument forward, caught now in an epistemological vicious circle: the written words say that the oral exposition is better suited than they are for the task of expounding esoteric ideas that should not be made explicit. The second defining aspect is that Moses de Salerno's reading is at one remove from the text on which he is commenting. He probably did not know any Arabic, and it appears that he was not familiar with the Greco-Arabic and Islamic sources that Maimonides had employed: his knowledge of the *Guide* came solely from Ibn Tibbon's translation. Though purists might object to a critical reading based not on the original but on a translation, the history of literary criticism has many examples to offer of the effectiveness of this secondhand procedure. In the twentieth century alone, Borges's readings of Homer and the Arab classics, George Steiner's of Dostoyevsky and Tolstoy, Harold Bloom's of García Márquez and Cervantes show that it is possible to have a keen illuminating insight without fluency in the language in which the books were originally written.

Another scholar attached to the court of Frederick II was the Scottish alchemist and philosopher Michael Scot, noted translator of Arabic and astrologer to the emperor. Because of his fame as a fortune-teller, Dante gave Scot a place in the infernal circle where the diviners are punished, and had Virgil say of him, "He truly knew the game of magic frauds."[14] An account (not alas supported by documentary proof) has it that Scot collaborated with Jacob ben Abba Mari ben Simson Anatoli, the French Jewish scholar who was also at Frederick's court and who translated the works of Averroës, on a Latin version of the *Guide* from Ibn Tibbon's Hebrew. Though an earlier Latin translation of the *Guide* was known to Christian scholars in the second quarter of the thirteenth century, there is no accurate information on the identity of its first translator or translators into Latin.

Unlike Moses de Salerno and Michael Scot, the thirteenth-century Spanish scholar Shem Tov ben Joseph ibn Falaquera certainly had direct access to Maimonides' *Guide* in the original Judeo-Arabic. His *Moreh ha-Moreh* (*A Guide to the Guide* or, more correctly, *A Guide to the Rebellious*) evinces erudite knowledge of Arabic and Arab philosophy, as well as of Jewish thought. His method consists in translating a passage from Maimonides' Judeo-Arabic text, departing often from Ibn Tibbon's version, and then appending its Islamic or Greek sources that sometimes contradict Maimonides' thought, and sometimes contradict one another. Ibn Falaquera argued that three preconditions were required for reading the *Guide:* knowledge of the Torah, knowledge of science, and having reached the age of forty. According to Ibn Falaquera, no amount of mashalim can replace the scientific knowledge that is necessary to understand certain passages in the *Guide*, and he rejects both the oral transmission and the posterior written discussion as valid instruments of enlightenment. Only in the moment in which the text is apprehended (in the blink of an eye) does the learning take place.

Another commentator, the fourteenth-century Catalan philosopher Moses de Narbonne, agreed with Ibn Falaquera, arguing that what he called "prophetic apprehensions" in the mashalim reached the reader in lightning flashes of revelation. But for this to take place, Moses de Narbonne noted, the reader must be "philosophically inclined."[15] Later scholars, such as the seventeenth-century Italian physician Yashar Mi-Qandia (a disciple of Galileo known as Joseph Delmedigo) disagreed, and, while considering Moses de Narbonne "one who possessed knowledge of gold encased in silver," accused him at the same time of betraying Maimonides' intentions by revealing too many of his esoteric secrets.[16]

Among the many noted commentators both Jewish and Arabic, one of the earliest scholars who read the *Guide* with an individual interpretative eye was the celebrated Kabbalist Abraham Abulafia, who, barely a generation after Maimonides' death, wrote three separate commentaries on the *Guide*. Abulafia considered the *Guide* a mystical stepping-stone on the path toward ecstatic revelation, though not as inspired or useful to the faithful as his own Kabbalistic texts. As an itinerant teacher, Abulafia greatly contributed to the distribution of the *Guide* throughout much of the Mediterranean world.[17]

In the early fourteenth century the French scholar Joseph Caspi wrote not one but two commentaries on the *Guide* (which might at one time have constituted a single work): *'Ammudei kesef* (Pillars of Silver) and *Maskiyot kesef* (Filigree of Silver). In the first, Caspi lists seven characteristics drawn from the *Guide* that define the perplexed reader for whom the work is intended. One, the student must be someone for whom religion has become "a habit of the soul"; two, he must be someone who believes in the infallible validity of the Torah; three, he must be perfect in the strength of his belief and traits of his character (character, adds Caspi, as defined by Aristotle); four, he must have studied philosophy and learned its value; five, his intellect must be always awake and in action; six, he must feel distressed by the outer appearance of the rules of law; seven, he must know enough of the equivocal terms in the Torah to catch a glimmer of their meaning. Caspi concludes that Maimonides' perplexed reader is like a man who has two wives, the Torah and his own intelligence. Having read in Genesis that God made man "in His image" (1:27), the man is perplexed because he realizes that God is not corporeal. His love for the first wife, the Torah, makes him believe in the literal meaning of the words; his intellect, the second wife, bids him consider the analogical sense. And so he is torn between the two and suffers from the uxorial quarrel without knowing how to go forward. Caspi suggests that the man's perplexity stems from not realizing that each wife has a different comprehension of the sacred words, and that both comprehensions are valid. The *Guide* helps the perplexed man understand that the two senses can be grasped simultaneously, without having to choose one over the other.[18]

In spite of all these considerations and reconsiderations, there were those who continued to reject Maimonides' approach to the Jewish faith. The fifteenth-century Portuguese scholar Isaac Abarbanel, a deeply read biblical exegete who integrated experiences from his own itinerant years into his learned commentaries, spent most his life arguing in volume after volume with the author of the *Guide*. Abarbanel was born in 1437 and died in Venice a year past the prescribed three score and ten after a life of wandering that led him to serve first the king of Naples and later the Venice doges. While expressing admiration for some of Maimonides' ideas, Abarbanel sternly objected to his principles of faith drawn from the Torah, which (in Abarbanel's opinion) the Rambam had mistakenly considered a science based on axioms from which everything else could be derived. Abarbanel argued that instead the Torah should be seen as complete in itself, God's work in which every detail is neither more nor less important than the next. Abarbanel also rejected Maimonides' Aristotelian notion that the soul constitutes a mere human potentiality, "surviving only to the extent that, through a life of study and contemplation, it is transformed into an acquired mind and is *actualized*."[19] The true view of the matter, Abarbanel decreed, was the statement in the Torah that says that the souls were not created at the time the bodies are formed, nor do their acquired concepts constitute their immortal part. The notion of the soul as mere potentiality, according to Abarbanel, "is a nonsensical falsehood and a repugnant opinion."[20] In the same categorical way, he rejected Maimonides' opinion on miracles, divine events which Abarbanel accepted in their entirety at face value. As to Maimonides' idea that each individual must seek a personal ethical path, Abarbanel argued against it that the reliance of an individual on his own reason usually leads him away from conventional morality by encouraging the assertion of individualistic standards and judgments.[21] Abarbanel, trying to depict the Rambam as a Kabbalistic mystic, declared trustworthy a legend of his time concerning Maimonides' supposed late recantation: "It has been heard that

Isaac Abarbanel, *Perush al Nevi'im Rishonim* (Bible Commentaries),
printed in 1687 in Hamburg, Gross Family Collection, Tel Aviv, B.358.
(Gross Family Collection Trust, Tel Aviv)

Maimonides wrote an epistle towards the end of his life that included the following confession: 'At the end of my days a man visited me and taught me things that, had I not learned them at the end of my life, and were it not for the fact that my works had already been spread throughout the world, I would have recanted them.'"[22]

In spite of criticisms like these, Maimonides continued to find readers not only amid the members of his faith, but also in the Gentile world. One of the best sellers of the Middle Ages was the thirteenth-century *Golden Legend* by Jacobus de Voragine, a compendium of the lives of saints and explanations of holy days that became the most popular source of hagiographic information. In the seventy-second chapter, discussing the distance between heaven and earth and between the several celestial spheres, Voragine justifies his assertions by referring to Maimonides: "As Rabbi Moses, the greatest of philosophers, reports."[23] Maimonides was understood to be an incontrovertible authority on celestial matters.

Maimonides was also read among fellow scholars throughout the Arab world, both Muslims and Christian Arabs. Among the latter, Al-Rashid Abu al-Khayr Ibn al-Tayyib admitted Maimonides into the Christian fold by declaring that because the author of the *Guide* was "a fully accomplished Jew" he must therefore be someone to whom God had revealed his laws, laws that were refined by the coming of Jesus.[24] Ibn al-Tayyib judged Maimonides something of an emulator of Christ.

It has been suggested by several (perhaps wishful) scholars, that Dante too read the *Guide* in a Latin translation and that he found in its pages inspiration for certain images in his *Commedia*. For instance, Dante's depiction of the serpent among the negligent rulers in canto 8 of *Purgatorio* might have been colored by Maimonides' interpretation of the serpent in Genesis as an allegory of human imagination or imaginative power that tempts Adam and Eve to fall for the deceit of the senses. In

Dante's *Purgatorio*, the serpent regularly appears at nightfall among the rulers, and is regularly chased away by two guardian angels with blunted swords. In the *Inferno*, the serpent is used as an image to depict the Messenger chasing away the froglike demons who bar Dante and Virgil from entrance to the City of Dis.[25] Human imagination, for Maimonides, has this double quality: negative in that it ties us to the earthly realm of the senses, and positive because it is through the imagination that the things of the world can appear to us as the enactment of God's will.[26]

One peculiar reader of both the *Commedia* and the *Guide* was Immanuel Romano, who was born in 1261 and died in 1335, an Italian Jewish poet and scholar who might have known and befriended Dante.[27] His Hebrew-language collection of stories in rhymed prose and poetry modeled on the *maqāma* (a tenth-century Arabic literary genre) became known as the *Mekhabarot Immanuel* (The Booklets of Immanuel) and consists of twenty-eight poems and their commentaries on subjects ranging from physical love to social interactions. Immanuel Romano is the only Jewish poet of the thirteenth century whose Italian lyrics are extant, surviving in six manuscripts. He is thought to have used the *Commedia* as his inspiration for the section called *Ha-Tofet ve-ha-'eden* (Hell and Paradise), in which a certain Daniel (a Hebraized version of "Dante") leads the pilgrim Immanuel through hell and heaven, where they meet both biblical and modern personalities. In the *Mekhabarot*, together with Dante-Daniel, Immanuel chose to address Maimonides and his *Guide*. Seemingly praising the Rambam by declaring that Maimonides' books are Immanuel's "queenly wives" while all others are merely his "concubines," Ishmael ironically criticizes several points in Maimonides' writings, pointing out what he considers errors and contradictions. Attempting to protect himself from accusations of blasphemy, Immanuel declared, "I've made in my time important poems . . . and he that thinks that they had

reached their aim—dreamt a dream."[28] The excuse proved use-
less: three centuries later, the great codifier of Jewish Law, Joseph Karo, banned the works of Immanuel Romano declaring
them to be heretical.

In 1418, Moses ben Isaac da Rieti, an Italian physician and
poet who became chief rabbi of the Jewish community of Rome
and later private doctor to Pope Pius II, attempted a project
similar to Immanuel Romano's, coupling the names of Dante
and Maimonides in an effort to honor and criticize both, together with several other illustrious poets and thinkers of the
past. Under the influence of Dante's *Commedia* and the verses
of Ibn Gabirol, Rieti wrote, at the age of twenty-four, a poem
describing a journey to Paradise in which, after an invocation
mirroring Dante's own, Rieti parodies Maimonides' *Thirteen
Principles of Faith* with nods toward Averroës, Avicenna, and many
others. Rieti gave his multi-layered poem the title *Mikdash Me'at*
(Little Sanctuary), in reference to Ezekiel 11:16: "I have indeed
removed them far among the nations, and have scattered them
among the countries, and I have become to them a diminished
sanctity [also translated "little sanctuary"] in the countries wither
they have gone." Rieti's poem became so popular that certain
sections of it were put to music and sung in the synagogues of
Italy.[29]

One of Dante's main intellectual sources was the thirteenth-
century church father Thomas Aquinas. Aquinas was certainly
familiar with the works of Maimonides, though it might be fair
to say of the saint's relationship to the Jewish master what has
been said of Dante's to Aquinas. "The essential thing is . . . for
us to notice the profound gulf that separates the actual nature
of the problem propounded by [one] from the apparently similar problem in [the other] to which it is often compared."[30]
Mainly, Aquinas concurs with Maimonides on the unknowability of God unless it is effected through his negative attributes.
In Maimonides' words, "We are only able to apprehend the

fact that He is, and cannot apprehend His quiddity."[31] For us to know God would be as if we tried to be God or, in other words, If I knew him I would be he. A number of times in his extensive work, Aquinas quoted directly from the *Guide*, calling the Rambam "Moyses Egyptius"; in the nineteenth century, the French scholar Émile Saisset argued that the *Guide* "announces and paves the way for Aquinas' *Summa Theologica*."[32] Though Aquinas at times disagrees with Maimonides, his own negative theology has a clear echo of the Jewish master's: "Since we cannot know what God is, but rather what He is not, we cannot consider how He is but how He is not."[33] Aquinas also agreed with Maimonides as to the necessity of withholding certain revelations from the unprepared: "There are other [truths] which, if openly presented, cause harm to those hearing them." And Aquinas adds, "If any subtleties are proposed to uncultivated people, these folk may find in the imperfect comprehension of them matter for error."[34]

The English theologian Alexander of Hales, in his vast *Summa Universae Theologiae*, a work completed by his students after his death in 1245, gives reverent attention to Ibn Gabirol's *Fountain of Life* (under the impression that he was not Jewish) and more reluctantly to Maimonides' *Guide*, both in Latin translations. Alexander takes from the *Guide* the assertion that there are two different forms of knowledge of God: one the knowledge per se, the other through God's work in the world; the former allows us to know him "face to face," the latter to see him "from behind." And he adds that Maimonides' presentation of Jewish judicial and ceremonial laws in the *Mishneh Torah* are useful for Christian observance, but although they have a certain spiritual value, coming as they do from outside the true faith, they should not be taken literally.[35]

A century after Maimonides, Robert Grosseteste, bishop of Lincoln and translator of Aristotle into Latin, was (scholars suggest) a reader of Maimonides. The problem is that the many references to the author of the *Guide* and the use of the Rambam's esoteric terminology, especially as regards astronomical considerations, appear only in Grosseteste's *Summa Philosophiae*, known now to be apocryphal, the work perhaps of his most famous student, Roger Bacon. Though at times disagreeing with a number of Maimonides' arguments, the author of the *Summa* (whoever he was) explicitly concurs with the author of the *Guide* in their mutual estimation of Aristotle as the supreme philosopher (though this was a commonplace at the time).[36] Was Bacon himself a reader of Maimonides? Though there are no references to Maimonides or the *Guide* in Bacon's acknowledged work, recent scholarship has suggested that Bacon "knew and used this work in the context of his discussion of many philosophical themes" and that he had probably acquired familiarity with Maimonides' ideas in the work of Thomas of Yorke that Bacon explicitly studied.[37]

A few decades after Bacon, the foremost English Franciscan theologian, John Duns Scotus, quoted Maimonides on the indemonstrability of God's singularity only to contradict him. At least in part, this choice of antagonist may be due to Duns Scotus's explicit anti-Semitism. Among other anti-Jewish measures, he advocated the forced baptism of Jewish children without their parents' permission "in order to save them."[38] Other Christian thinkers were less emphatic in their prejudice. The Avignon pope John XXII, who in 1317 issued a bull ordering all Jews to wear an identifying badge, approvingly quoted in a later bull a passage of the *Guide* concerning God's unity, noting that in Maimonides' words, God's being is One "by virtue of a true Oneness, so that no composition whatever is to be found in Him, and no possibility of division any way whatever."[39]

In the fourteenth century, the German theologian Eckhart von Hochheim, commonly known as Meister Eckhart, whose works were banned by the same Pope John XXII, frequently referred to Maimonides in his vast Latin corpus. To take just one example, in Eckhart's *Opus tripartitum*, Maimonides' name appears 119 times, second only to Saint Augustine's and Aristotle's. It can perhaps be said that Meister Eckhart saw in Maimonides his Jewish soulmate. His attitude toward Maimonides' ideas is embracingly positive, particularly in regards to Maimonides' metaphysics and his negative theology. Meister Eckhart quotes approvingly Maimonides' moral assertions, his scientific and cosmological interpretations of certain Mosaic passages, and many of the Rambam's interpretations of the Talmud and the Torah, showing how closely Meister Eckhart had read the *Guide* (in Latin translation). Maimonides' arguments regarding the unknowability of God strongly influenced Eckhart's denial of any epistemological relation between the Creator and his creation, and therefore of any kind of similarity. Akin too is Eckhart's proclaimed intention to lead his audience not from ignorance to philosophy but from the ecstatic to the intellectual realm, which (as Maimonides had stated) is not in everyone's reach. At the conclusion of one of his sermons, Meister Eckhart warns his audience, "Now I beg you to be disposed to what I say, for I say to you in everlasting truth that if you are unlike this truth of which we want to speak, you cannot understand me." And he concludes, "There is no need to understand this. Whoever does not understand what I have said, let him not burden his heart with it; for as long as a man is not equal to this truth, he will not understand these words, for this is a truth beyond speculation that comes immediately from the heart of God."[40]

Three centuries after Meister Eckhart, John Milton, sufficiently conversant in Hebrew to read in that language the Old Testament and the rabbinical commentaries, drew for his *Paradise Lost* on Maimonides' "satanic serpent" described in the *Guide* as seducing Eve through lust ("it cast pollution into her"), and also on his depiction of the Fall of Adam not as a descent from innocence into sin but as the ascent of passion to overcome reason.[41] Maimonides provided Milton not only with poetic in-spiration but also with practical conjugal advice. Milton found in Maimonides' *Guide* a religious justification for the poet's in-tention of divorcing his wife Mary Powell. "Hence it is that the Rabbis and Maimonides, famous among the rest, in a book of his, tells us that divorce was permitted to Moses to preserve the peace and quiet in the family."[42]

Isaac Newton was probably influenced by Maimonides' writings in his arguments concerning prophecy not as a mysti-cal illumination but as the achievement of truth through the application of reason. This is why the economist John May-nard Keynes called Newton "a Judaic monotheist of the school of Maimonides."[43] The editor of Newton's theological writings concurred, and noted that "there is evidence of Newton's inter-est in Maimonides, whose *Guide for the Perplexed* argued that 'God is a free cause, but a rational one, his rationality lying in the homogeneity of creation.' . . . Newton agreed with Mai-monides that 'The doors of interpretation are not closed,' and, like him, was a moralist and a rationalist, but not a skeptic."[44] It would have been unlikely for Newton to be unaware of Mai-monides' work since at least from the seventeenth century on, Maimonides was considered an essential author in any Euro-pean learned library. When the Jewish printer Mordechai Tama produced in 1765 in Amsterdam a collection of thirty-eight pre-viously unpublished *responsa* by Maimonides, translated from the original Judeo-Arabic into Hebrew, it became one of the most important Hebrew books printed in the eighteenth century.[45]

The English scholar James Harrington, author of a very readable utopian novel published in 1656, *The Commonwealth of Oceana*, drew heavily on the *Mishneh Torah* to define a form of patrician government ruled by popular vote and overseen by a tribunal of judges ordained through a system almost identical to the one set out by Maimonides. In addition, a contemporary of Harrington's, the Anglican bishop and sermonist Jeremy Tay-

Autograph responsum of Maimonides, written in a mixture of Hebrew and Judeo-Arabic, twelfth century, Cairo, British Library, London, Or. 5519 B. (Photo: Album/Alamy Stock Photo) lor, was a keen reader of Maimonides, and frequently quoted the *Guide* in support of his own rationalistic account of divinity. Perhaps the title of one of Taylor's most important books, *Ductor dubitantium*, is a paraphrase of the 1520 Latin translation of the *Guide, Dux seu director dubitantium aut perplexorum.*

Gottfried Wilhelm Leibniz shared with Maimonides the adamant belief that reason held a central role in matters of faith, particularly with regards to the conception of the soul, the nature of angels, and the limits of human knowledge. Leibniz read and annotated Maimonides' *Guide* in the Latin translation published in 1629 when Leibniz was just an adolescent. However, the young Leibniz had only a vague understanding of the differences between Islamic and Jewish beliefs. "Mohamed," he wrote, "found means to fill Asia and Africa with a religion which is scarcely different from that of the Jews except in its ceremonies."[46] This led him to imagine that he could reach an understanding of Islamic thought through the *Guide*. In spite of considering Maimonides a representative of "the Abrahamic faiths" that had disdained Christian belief, Leibniz found several points of agreement with him on basic theological notions. In general terms, Leibniz concurred with Maimonides on the tenet that the universe is essentially of one piece under the rule of the One Author. Leibniz argued that the conscious human soul, a self-sufficient and self-contained microcosm (or monad, as Leibniz calls it), is the essence of a human being. Maimonides had stated in the *Guide* that if human beings are microcosms, each striving to know God, then they are microcosms submitted to an overall cosmic rulership because, just as a person without the rule of rational faculties would perish, the universe itself would perish without its Lord. Leibniz explains this with a cubist example: "And just as the same town, when looked at from different sides, appears quite different and is, as it were, multiplied in perspective, so also it happens that because of the infinite number of simple substances, it is as if there were as many different universes, which are however but different perspective representations of a single universe from the different point of view of each monad."[47] Leibniz attributes a soul to everything that is capable of perception, but adds that the human soul is gifted with keener perception and with the unique power of memory. "It is the knowledge of necessary and eternal truths that distinguishes us from the mere animals and gives us Reason and the sciences, raising us to the knowledge of ourselves and of God."[48] This knowledge, both for Maimonides and for Leibniz, is necessarily limited: only Supreme Reason possesses unlimited understanding.

In 1621, the Oxford scholar Robert Burton, in his *Anatomy of Melancholy*, attributed to "Rabbi Moses" the rebuttal of "Epicureal tenets, tending to looseness of life, luxury and atheism," which Burton also rejected. Burton might also have been aware, through indirect reference or through his own reading of the Latin translation, of Maimonides' writings on depression (or melancholy) and his recommendation that the sickness should be cured by means of the five senses. At the same time, John Donne approvingly quoted Maimonides, whom (as we have said) he called "the saddest and soundest of the Hebrew Rabbins" in one of his sermons, concerning the Rambam's notion that the will of God becomes manifest in his creation.[49]

This last is an idea that spoke, a century later, to Bishop George Berkeley. The founder of the idealism school does not mention Maimonides by name but shares with him specific notions such as the nature of angels—or "intelligences" as they both call them, following Avicenna. Berkeley's arguments on the nature of God coincide with Maimonides' in recognizing its unknowability except as an idea. Maimonides postulates God as the *fons et origo* of everything, including himself, and suggests that human beings can only approach knowledge of the divine through either illuminating grace or God's ideas put into ac-

tion in the world. In his attack on representationalist material-
ism, Berkeley argues that God is an infinite spirit that causes
our sensory ideas to emerge; they in turn are responsible for
our perception of the world. It is this vicarious perception of
reality that according to Berkeley's idealism brings the qualities
of the world that we call real into existence. The world depends
on God's perceptions, but we share only the perceptions which
correspond to or are included in his volitions about what we
should or can perceive.[50]

In 1677 Baruch Spinoza died in The Hague. A year later,
his revolutionary book *Ethics, Demonstrated in Geometrical Order*
was published in Amsterdam, a work that in the opinion of
G. W. F. Hegel, author of *Phenomenology of Spirit*, was the cornerstone of modern philosophy, "so that it may really be said,
you are either a Spinozist or not a philosopher at all."[51] Brought
up in the Portuguese Jewish community of Amsterdam, Spinoza worked all his life as a lens grinder and died of lung disease, probably due to the glass dust he had inhaled daily. When
still in his twenties, Spinoza publicly questioned the authenticity of certain passages in the Hebrew Bible, opinions deemed
so heretical that he was officially expelled from the community
by the Talmud Torah Congregation of his city; a few years before his death at the age of forty-four, and for the same reasons,
Spinoza's work was placed on the Catholic Church's *Index of
Forbidden Books*. Spinoza opposed the mind-body dualistic vision of René Descartes, and argued for the existence of an im-
personal God, while applying logic and reason to deny elements of the religious dogma, such as the resurrection, divine
providence, the immortality of the soul, and the performance
of miracles. These arguments have points in common with certain tenets of Maimonides; however, to a much greater extent,
the views of Spinoza contradict those of the author of the *Guide*.
Spinoza deemed Maimonides' interpretative theological methods dangerous because, in his view, they allowed for readings

contrary to the spirit of the text. The Brazilian scholar Marilena Chaui, comparing the opposition to Maimonides by his contemporaries to that provoked by Spinoza in his five centuries later, suggests a similarity in the reasons of the opposers. Maimonides, as mentioned, was vilified for his allegorical interpretations of the Holy Word, and Spinoza for his literal one. All the same, both thinkers believed that a philosophical approach could provide a path to faith, leading us "to the infinite map of Him who" (as Borges described in a poem on Spinoza) "is all His stars."[52]

Spinoza believed that if read correctly the message of the Bible is a simple moral one: to know and love God, and to love one's neighbor as oneself. In this he agreed with Maimonides. In the *Mishneh Torah* the Rambam had written, "Duty demands of every person to love his fellow man as himself."[53] The sentiment has ancient roots. In the first century BCE the rabbi Hillel had stated much the same. The Talmud says that a prospective convert came to Hillel and to another rabbi, Shammai, and asked them to teach him the essence of the Torah while standing on one foot. The second rabbi dismissed the man as a fool, but Hillel stood on one foot and answered: "Don't do unto your neighbor what you would not want done unto you. This is the whole of the Law: the rest is commentary."[54]

More important, in his opposition to Maimonides' belief, Spinoza argued that the message of the Torah is not to instruct but to compel obedience, and to give rules for proper behavior. "Scriptural doctrine," Spinoza wrote, "contains not abstruse speculation or philosophic reasoning, but very simple matters able to be understood by the most sluggish mind." The only guidance the faithful can expect from the Bible is an inspiration to obey the word of God and to treat others with mercy and justice. For this, Spinoza believed, familiarity with Scripture was not even necessary. "He who, while unacquainted with these writings, nevertheless knows by the natural light that there is a God having the attributes we have recounted, and who also pursues a true way of life, is altogether blessed."[55] This love of God elicited through the intellect is for Spinoza equivalent to Aristotle's eudaemonia. It is the extent to which we can aspire in our thirst of knowledge: it coincides with the measure of our virtue, our happiness, our well-being, our autonomy, and our salvation. Wisdom and virtue, happiness, self-fulfillment, and salvation, are for Spinoza all one and the same.

Both Spinoza and Maimonides came once again to the forefront of philosophical debate a century after Spinoza's death. German Christian intellectuals of the eighteenth century, among them Johann Gottfried Herder, Gotthold Ephraim Lessing, and Immanuel Kant, agreed in considering Judaism a mere set of religious laws, as proven in their eyes by Maimonides' *Mishneh Torah*, while Christianity (on whose tenets they mostly disagreed) was a universal religion to which the Jews should turn either through faith or through reason if they wished to be saved.

These intellectuals, seeking to prove the overall validity of reason, found that Spinoza's arguments provided an alternative to both atheism and deism. At least three of Spinoza's ideas (which they could also find, albeit less dogmatically stated, in Maimonides) strongly appealed to them: the unity of everything in the universe, the cyclical progress of events, and the ineffable nature of the material and the spiritual world. These points became the core of a widely extended debate on what was seen as Spinoza's "pantheistic" conception of God (that the universe is identical to its Maker: *Deus sive natura*, "God or nature"), an idea opposed to Maimonides' argument that God's nature is itself unknowable, but that the human intellect can grasp his presence in his worldly acts.[56] This *Pantheismusstreit* (as the debate was called in Germany) began as a personal disagreement between two German Jews, Friedrich Heinrich Jacobi and Moses Mendelssohn, over what they understood to be Lessing's understanding of Spinoza's arguments: an assessment twice removed. Mendelssohn argued that even if Lessing had, as Jacobi supposed, truly believed in Spinoza's metaphysical conclusions and his rationalistic critique of religion, this belief should be taken with a pinch of salt, because "throughout his life Lessing preferred to hear an incorrect doctrine defended skillfully rather than hear a truth defended with shallow reasoning." Mendelssohn accepted Lessing's confession of Spinozism as sincere, but responded to Jacobi by saying that Lessing's "refined" Spinozism was less adamant than the "master ironist" (Lessing) had led Jacobi to believe.[57] Lessing responded to Mendelssohn's criticism by turning the philosopher into the saintly protagonist of his 1779 ecumenical play *Nathan the Wise*.

In 1785, Jacobi published his exchanges with Mendelssohn. Four years earlier, in a commentary on the Pentateuch, Mendelssohn had argued that Jews are obliged to follow the prescribed laws—laws that were written out in the Pentateuch but also the Oral Law "derived through argumentation according to rules of scriptural explication established through tradition"— because "we are obligated to perform God's will."[58] The conclusions of these arguments, Mendelssohn pointed out, were set by Maimonides "in a comprehensive book of law," which, however, omitted different opinions and conflicting arguments. Because these conclusions encountered considerable opposition, said Mendelssohn, they did not attain the authority of a code of law. In the midst of the debate, seeking to define philosophically the position of human beings in relation to their Creator according to the tenets of Judaism, and torn between Maimonides' unknowable Maker and Spinoza's "absolutely infinite" divinity, Mendelssohn chose a middle path: God knows human imperfection, but does not possess it; that is why, precisely because of our human imperfections, we are distinct from God. Mendelssohn believed that Jewish worship of God should be a private practice, limited to the synagogue and the home, so as not to create obstacles to the integration of the Jews in European society. This should be done, Mendelssohn believed, even at the cost of rejecting much of the medieval Jewish scholastic tradition.[59]

Moses Mendelssohn was the central figure of the Jewish Enlightenment of the eighteenth century. The movement, called Haskalah (after the Hebrew word *sekhel*, "intellect," or *haskalah*, "education, knowledge"), centered around the Königsberg-Berlin journal *Ha-Meassef* (The Collector). The first issue of *Ha-Meassef* appeared in 1783, three years after Emperor Joseph II of Austria issued the Edict of Tolerance that would allow Jews the choice of setting up their own schools or enrolling their children in Catholic institutions. The editors of the journal chose to call themselves the Maskilim, "scholars in the field of Jewish thought," and looked to the works of Maimonides for guidance. The Maskilim saw in Maimonides a brilliant precursor of the enlightened Jew, a secular hero, but were less impressed by his theological arguments. Mendelssohn instead was very impressed, and his interest in Maimonides became a lifelong affair.

As a young adolescent, Mendelssohn had read Maimonides' *Mishneh Torah* as part of his Talmudic studies, and he was introduced early on to the mysteries of the *Guide*. Mendelssohn himself reveals that he studied Maimonides' books "day and night" and that they "turned my days of sorrow into days of joy, and if they did me wrong by weakening my body, they repaid me sevenfold by healing my soul through their lofty ideas."[60] Mendelssohn believed (and found this belief confirmed in the words of the Rambam) that logic is independent of all value outside itself. However, Maimonides had prescribed philosophical beliefs as religious precepts, and Mendelssohn could not bring himself to accept the tenet that faith could be subject to religious legislation. If belief could be legislated, Mendelssohn argued, human power to reach essential rational truths would be radically weakened. The tolerance sought for, and defended after Joseph II's edict, by the members of the Jewish Enlightenment could not justify elitist notions of privilege, and the Maskilim could not bring themselves to accept that only the Jews, if they followed the Law (which Mendelssohn labeled "revealed legislation"), could be saved. "Can it be," Mendelssohn wrote, "that all of the earth's inhabitants, excepting us, will go to their destruction unless they believe in the Torah which was given as a heritage for Jacob alone?"[61] The egalitarian society in which Mendelssohn believed was not envisaged in the *Guide:* on the contrary. The parable of the secluded palace in the *Guide* makes it clear that only a select few will reside within its walls. But all readers can, if keen enough, find in almost any text the meaning they are seeking. The Jewish intelligentsia of the Enlightenment sought and found support for their liberal views in both Maimonides' legal and his mystical writings. The Rambam's defense of science and secular study could be understood as upholding the Maskilim's enlightened educational programs, his political belief in the power of the monarch could be used in support of their willingness to accommodate the Jews in the new imperial society, his stress on the importance of speaking any language fluently could be seen as bolstering the Maskilim's insistence on learning not only the Hebrew *safa b'rurah* (pure speech) but also the pure German *Sprache*. And even (in spite of his strict definition of what constitutes a Jew) Maimonides' acknowledgment that human beings all share equal intelligence differentiated only by circumstance and education could be understood to uphold their wished-for egalitarian society. And when Maimonides' views could not be made to suit their purposes, the Maskilim merely ignored them, silently removing a word or two from a quotation. Where Maimonides states that the purpose of the world is the existence of good and wise men, and that the rest of humanity was created to keep the wise ones company, the Maskilim added, "and also so that members of the different groups should help one another."[62] Thanks to Mendelssohn and his fellow intellectuals, Maimonides became a stellar figure of the Jewish Enlightenment.

Mendelssohn himself was turned into a fictional character in a curious satire that appeared in the Haskalah's *Ha-Meassef.* The piece, by the biblical commentator and translator Aaron Wolfsohn of Halle, is in some ways reminiscent of Rieti's poem on Dante and his *Commedia.* It is entitled *Siha be-Eretz ha-Hayyim* (Discussions in Heaven) and describes the encounter in heaven of Maimonides with the recently deceased Mendelssohn, together with a stereotypical conservative rabbi named P'loni, a conflation of "Anonymous" (*Ploni* in Hebrew) and "Polish" (*Polani*). The rabbi, criticizing Mendelssohn for his views, says that he is a devout follower of Maimonides, whereby Maimonides intervenes, snubs the rabbi, whose archaic Hebrew he professes not to understand, and engages Mendelssohn in a lively dialogue attacking P'loni's retrograde ideas.[63]

The other Enlightenment, the period known traditionally and presumptuously as the Age of Reason, counted a number of Gentile admirers of Maimonides and his work. In France, Denis Diderot dedicated a lengthy article of his subversive *Encyclopédie* to the author of the *Guide* in which Maimonides is compared to Diogenes among the Greeks because "he was the first of the doctors who did more than jest among the Jews." Diderot goes on to say that Maimonides believed that the sin of idolatry ceases to be a sin when committed in secret, thereby distorting Maimonides' actual opinion that when a person's life is at risk, apostasy can be excused as a strategy of survival. "His works were received with much applause," Diderot concedes. "Nevertheless, it must be confessed that he often had quite arbitrary ideas and, having studied metaphysics, he made great use of it." After giving a few random examples of Maimonides' statements taken out of context, Diderot concludes, "All this is quite subtle, but doesn't remove the difficulty and doesn't reveal the true meaning of God's words." Diderot himself was not much inclined to seek a true comprehension of esoteric matters. His own definition of God is not much more than a bon mot: "a father who cares much about his apples and very little about his children."[64]

Voltaire, Diderot's contemporary, appears to have had a deeper understanding and appreciation of Maimonides. He saw in Maimonides an early representative of the logic and reason that Voltaire judged lacking in most religious discourse, and admired Maimonides for being a philosopher who pointed out contradictions and impossibilities in the biblical narrative, insisting that such fantastical passages should be read allegorically. And while dismissing or refusing to consider Maimonides' theological arguments proper, Voltaire praised the author of the *Guide*, saying that, after him, "the Jews had intelligible books, and were therefore dangerous [to Christians]" because, according to Voltaire, Maimonides had reminded the Gentiles of their debt to Judaism. To make his point, Voltaire put words in Maimonides' mouth: "We are your fathers, our writings are yours, our books are read aloud in your churches, our songs are sung there. And you respond by looting them, and chasing them away, and condemning them to the gallows."[65] This quotation is nowhere to be found in the works of the Rambam.

The history of the *Guide* in Hebrew follows a different path from that of its Latin translations. The first printed edition of the Hebrew version of the *Guide* appeared in Rome in 1480; a second followed in Lisbon seventeen years later, shortly before the Jewish exile from Portugal. Two more editions followed, one in Venice in 1551 and another in the Mantuan town of Sabionetta in 1553.[66] Almost two centuries would go by before the next Hebrew printing, and after that the *Guide* would have to wait yet another century for a revised and corrected edition to appear, this time in Berlin, with commentaries from two of the most distinguished scholars of the Jewish Enlightenment: the Polish scholar and poet Isaac ha-Levy Satanow annotated parts II and III, and the Lithuanian philosopher Solomon Maimon part I. In his autobiography, the latter explains that he held Maimonides in such high esteem that he changed his name from Shlomo ben Yehoshua to Maimon, and that whenever he feared that temptation would lead him away from true wisdom, he would say, "I swear by the reverence which I owe to my great teacher, Rabbi Moses ben Maimon, not to do this act."[67] Apparently this was sufficient to restrain him.

Maimon and other Jewish liberal thinkers sought to prove that certain isolated Maimonidean doctrines had found their way into the philosophy of Immanuel Kant, and soon proposed "an inherent congruency between major parts of Kantian philosophy and the teachings of the *Guide*."[68] It is true that like Maimonides, Kant believed that reason is the source of morality. The Jewish enthusiasts went farther. They argued that Kant's *Ding-an-sich* (a thing as it is in itself, not mediated through perception by the senses or conceptualization, and therefore unknowable) and Maimonides' concept of a God known only through his negative attributes both constituted a single common postulate of practical reason that blossomed into "the highest ethical principle." According to these Jewish thinkers, Kant had attempted to find a middle ground between rationalists and empiricists; that is to say, in terms of the knowledge of God and the knowledge of the Law, the assurance of how to conduct oneself properly in the world. Between those who demanded material proof of God's existence and those who trusted that they could reason their way into believing in him, Kant undertook to lay aside these claims—the existence or nonexistence of God—and judge the question indemonstrable, something that neither philosophy nor theology could prove or disprove.[69] If Spinoza is the thinker behind Kant's purely moral defense of religion, after being shorn of its intellectual, philosophical, and scientific claims, Maimonides is at the root of Kant's notions of ethics and morality. This does not mean that Kant sides uncritically with either thinker. Spinoza saw moral rules as relative to time and place. Kant, countering these claims, argued that morality was an a priori principle, universal and necessary. The supreme good (the Aristotelian notion embraced by Maimonides) is for Kant dictated by this tenet, which requires that everyone aspire to happiness in proportion to each person's moral achievement. Maimonides insisted that from a religious point of view, the philosophical tradition is more important than the moral one.[70] Kant opposed this concept by limiting the reaches of pure reason through the norms of practical reason. *Pace* Maimon and his fellow intellectuals, Kant and Maimonides seem to be at opposite ends in their definitions of the common or separate fields of metaphysics and theology.

The twentieth century found new readers of Maimonides among some of its greatest writers: Franz Kafka, James Joyce, Jorge Luis Borges. Kafka discovered the figure of Maimonides as a canonized Jewish hero in Heinrich Graetz's idiosyncratic *History of the Jews;* later on, Kafka found a more nuanced version of the Rambam in the books of the Talmudist Jacob Fromer, through whom he learned that the author of the *Guide* had been considered a heretic by orthodox Judaism, "hopping between two opinions" as Fromer put it, quoting Elijah's reproof of the unfaithful people of Israel in 1 Kings 18:21.[71] In Solomon Maimon's autobiography, Kafka read an extensive account of Maimonides as a man who, on his lifelong quest to find his Jewish identity, had explored several cultures—Greek, Arabic, and Jewish—much as Kafka had explored, beyond his own Jewish culture, the cultures of Christian Europe, the New World, and the "exotic" Far East. What seems to have interested Kafka in Maimonides is the Rambam's ability to straddle two fields of Jewish thought—the strict legal field of the *Mishneh Torah* and the metaphysical field of the *Guide*—without embracing the idea of a Promised Land concretely, in the political present of the thirteenth century. In the twentieth century, Kafka followed a similar strategy. Kafka's borderless curiosity, which permeated all his writings, prevented him (he said) from becoming a Zionist like his friend Max Brod. "All such writing," Kafka confessed, meaning his own efforts, "might have developed into a new secret doctrine, a Kabbalah, if Zionism had not intervened." He clarified this categorically in a 1916 letter to his beloved Felice Bauer: "I am not a Zionist."[72] Kafka found in the writings of Maimonides certain concepts *against which* to reflect. For example, discussing the subject of judgment and trial in the *Guide* in reference to the book of Job, Maimonides declares that the notion of trial is "one of the greatest difficulties of the Law." He then gives the popular definition of trial: "God sends down calamities upon an individual, without their having been preceded by a sin, in order that his reward be increased."[73] It is not difficult to see in Kafka's most famous novel an echo of Maimonides' words.

Maimonides appears as a less obvious influence in the work of another formidable twentieth-century writer, James Joyce. When Joyce decided to translate the Homeric Odysseus into the son of an Irish Jew wandering the streets of Dublin, he sought classical Jewish authorities to bolster Leopold Bloom's reluctant Judaism. In the Ithaca chapter of *Ulysses*, written in what Joyce's biographer Richard Ellman called a "form of mathematical catechism," Bloom and Stephen Dedalus engage in a parodic dialectic dialogue, in a give-and-take Talmudic style. Discussing the pedagogical method of "indirect suggestion implicating self-interest," Maimonides appears as one of three "examples of postexilic eminence" (i.e., in Jewish history between the sixth century BCE exile from Babylon and the first century CE): "Three seekers of the pure truth, Moses of Egypt, Moses Maimonides, author of *More Nebukim* (Guide of the Perplexed) and Moses Mendelssohn of such eminence that from

Moses (of Egypt) to Moses (Mendelssohn) there arose none like Moses (Maimonides)."[74]

Jorge Luis Borges, keen reader of Jewish theology, the Talmud, and the Kabbalah, had certainly read Maimonides, at least the *Guide*, and the entry on Maimonides in the eleventh edition of the *Encyclopaedia Britannica*. He had also read a number of histories of Jewish thought and religion—Henry Hart Milman's *History of the Jews*, Marcus Brann's *Geschichte der Juden und ihrer Literatur*, Fritz Mauthner's *Ausgewählte Schriften*, Étienne Gilson's *La philosophie du Moyen Age*, Nahum N. Glatzer's *In Time and Eternity: A Jewish Reader*, and especially Isaac Husik's *A History of Mediaeval Jewish Philosophy*—that discuss Maimonides' work and influence.[75] These books are annotated in Borges's hand and show his interest in Maimonides' arguments and parables, and some of Maimonides' ideas were translated into Borges's own fictions. For instance, Maimonides' assertion that God's knowledge is not comprehensible in terms of human intelligence is evident in Borges's "Argumentum ornithologicum":

> I close my eyes and I see a flock of birds. The vision lasts a second or perhaps less; I don't know how many birds I have seen. Was it a definite or an indefinite number? The problem involves that of the existence of God. If God exists, the number is definite, because God knows how many birds I have seen. If God does not exist, than the number is indefinite, because no one could have kept count. In that case, I saw less than ten birds (let's say) and more than one, but I did not see nine, eight, seven, six, five, four, three, two birds. I saw a number between ten and one that is not nine, eight, seven, six, five, etc. That whole number is inconceivable; ergo, God exists.[76]

Only once in his writings does Borges mention Maimonides by name. In the story "The Secret Miracle," the protagonist, the Czech playwright Jaromir Hladík, about to be shot by the Gestapo, has requested God in a silent prayer to grant him time to finish his last play. In a dream, he hears that his request has been granted. Then Hladík remembers that "the dreams of men belong to God and that Maimonides had written that the words in a dream are divine when they are clear and distinct and the speaker cannot be seen."[77] Perhaps it is a sign of Borges's inventive memory that this precise reference has not been traced to any of Maimonides' writings.

Several of the twentieth century's greatest scientific minds have been aware of Maimonides' ideas and in some cases tacitly echoed them in their own writings. In 1935, at the Maimonides Jubilee Celebration, Albert Einstein declared that Maimonides had exerted "a crucial and fruitful influence" on both his contemporaries and "later generations" but that he could not count himself among the Rambam's disciples. Five years earlier, he had written to his friend A. Geller that "unfortunately I have not read Maimonides." There was, however, a book by Maimonides in Einstein's library: Michael Friedländer's 1881 English translation of the *Guide* in a 1946 reprint: we don't know if Einstein finally read it or merely kept it on his shelf. And yet Einstein, if he eventually read the *Guide*, must have felt a kinship with Maimonides in that his personal theology declared that "knowledge of God can be obtained by observing the visible processes of nature, with the proviso that the manifestation of the divine in the universe is only partially comprehensible to the human intellect."[78] But maybe this was simply a happy coincidence of thought.

In 1939, Sigmund Freud, in *Moses and Monotheism*, in a then-unpublished section that he sent to be read at the Fifteenth International Psychoanalytic Congress in Paris, addressed the question of the Torah as the key identifying symbol of the Jewish people: "The political misfortune of the [Jewish] nation taught them to appreciate the only possession they had retained, their Scripture, at its true value. Immediately after the destruction of the Temple by Titus, Rabbi Yochanan ben Zakkai asked for permission to open at Yabneh the first school for the study of the Torah. From now on it was the Holy Book and the intellectual effort applied to it that kept the people together."[79] Long before Freud, Maimonides had stated the importance of studying the Torah as one of his principles. A triad of American scholars postulated that the author of the *Guide* was a precursor of Freud not only in the centrality of the Torah in defining Jewish identity but principally because of Maimonides' concern with "the healing of the soul and its activities." According to these scholars, Freud was indebted to "Maimonides' distinctively psychological version of intellectual mysticism."[80]

Though there appears to be a certain similarity between Maimonides' interpretation of dreams and that of Freud, privileging words over images in dreams, there is unfortunately no documentary proof of Freud basing any of his theories on the writings of Maimonides. However, as Freud himself acknowledged, "There are a number of similar processes among those which the analytic investigation of mental life has made known to us."[81] Maimonides' *Guide* could be one of them.

Freud's colleague and later dissenter Carl Gustav Jung became interested in Maimonides for different reasons. If Freud saw in Maimonides someone who had recognized in the Torah a central tenet of the Jews' identity, and possibly a precursor of his own theories on the interpretation of dreams, Jung found in Maimonides a congenial reader of symbols and a fellow practitioner of the language of ambiguity that might help free interpretative statements from a dogmatic or definitive imprint. Maimonides' language in the *Guide*, intended to shed light but not constrain certain esoteric aspects of Scripture, has similarities with Jung's own. Seeking in the science of alchemy, derided since the eighteenth century, an imagistic or metaphorical language to address aspects of the human psyche beyond a curtailing clinical vocabulary, Jung wrote that "its wealth of symbols gives us an insight into an endeavour of the human mind which could be compared to a religious rite, an *opus divinum*." However, Jung made clear, "the alchemical opus was not a collective activity rigorously defined as to its form and content, but rather, despite the similarities of their fundamental principles, an individual undertaking on which the adept staked his whole soul for the transcendental purpose of producing a *unity*."[82] This mirrors, perhaps unwittingly, Maimonides' statement, repeated many times, in the *Guide* that the highest perfection to which an individual can aspire is intellectual, and consists in staking his whole soul for the transcendental purpose of ascertaining in divine matters everything that can be ascertained.[83] Jung also found in Maimonides' Talmudic and Kabbalistic sources certain retellings of the biblical stories, such as Adam in the Garden writing a book on trees and plants, and the symbolic meaning of Leviathan in the book of Job.[84] Jung says, "We can see from the example of Leviathan how the great 'fish' gradually split into its opposite, after having itself been the opposite of the highest God and hence his shadow, the embodiment of his evil side." And Jung adds in a footnote: "Perhaps an echo of this psychological development, may be found in the views of Moses Maimonides."[85]

One of Freud's disciples, Jacques Lacan, after studying Maimonides' *Guide* and placing Freud's arguments in a linguistic-historical context, argued that before considering the foundational importance of Scripture (which both Maimonides and Freud embraced) one first had to acknowledge that which he called the Book's Author, "the primary signifier": that is to say, the Hebrew name of God. "Here is someone," Lacan declared, "who satisfies that position, and whom I am going to name without hesitation, because he seems to me to be essential to the interest that we analysts should bring to Hebraic history. It is, perhaps, inconceivable that psychoanalysis could have been born anywhere else than in this tradition. Freud was born into it, and he insists on this fact, as I have stressed, that for making advances in the field he has discovered he only truly has confidence in these Jews who have known how to read for quite a long time and who live—this is the Talmud—on the reference to a text. He whom I am going to name, who, or which, actualizes this radical position of ferocious ignorance, has a name—it's Yahweh himself."[86]

The British philosopher Michael Lewis has argued that Lacan's psychoanalytical approach to symbols should be supplemented by Jacques Derrida's philosophical examination of language. Derrida rarely mentions Maimonides in his philosophical writings, and when he does, it is mainly to argue against the intellectuals of the Jewish Enlightenment who rallied Maimonides to their cause. Derrida, however, embraced Maimonides' negative theology in his 1993 essay "Sauf le nom."[87]

The French philosopher Emmanuel Levinas, on the other hand, had Maimonides as a constant reference in his work: in the *Levinas Concordance* the name of Maimonides appears some sixty times.[88] Levinas sought in the field of ethics a "first philosophy" (a position traditionally held by metaphysics or theology) and found early on in the writings of Maimonides a sympathetic correspondent. But in later years, Levinas became more ambivalent toward the author of the *Guide,* nevertheless sharing with him concepts of creativity and freedom of action limited under the Law. Of great importance to Levinas, as it was for Derrida, was Maimonides' position regarding the impossibility of defining the Godhead in positive terms; from Maimonides' negative theology Levinas developed what can be called an ethical negative theology.[89] To Maimonides' warning in the *Guide,* "Know that when you make an affirmation ascribing another thing to Him, you become more remote from Him in two respects: one of them is that everything you affirm is a perfection only with reference to us, and the other is that He does not possess a thing other than His essence," Levinas answers, "To approach the Other in conversation is to welcome his expression, in which at each instant he overflows the idea, a thought would carry away from it. It is therefore to receive from the Other beyond the capacity of the I, which means exactly: to have the idea of infinity. But this also means: to be taught."[90] Levinas enriches Maimonides' concept of the Unaffirmable with the argument that this same unaffirmability has the power to teach us that very condition.

The influence of Maimonides has been sought and found in many unlikely places, sometimes as a circumstantial mirroring of philosophical outlooks, sometimes as a startling coincidence. Though there is no evident link between Maimonides' Judaism and the religions of Asia, scholars have found parallels (somewhat forced, perhaps, considering Maimonides' conviction of the privileged status of the Jews) between, for instance, Maimonides' empathy toward the exiled outsider, and that of other philosophers in exile. One such scholar has suggested that Maimonides' concept of the Other was founded on his experience of the thirteenth-century Jewish diaspora, and that this is expressed in similar terms in the philosophy of the twelfth-century Japanese monk Shinran, founder of the Jodo Shinshu or True Pure Land Buddhism.[91] Another example put forward is that of Shinran's contemporary, the Chinese Confucian scholar Zhu Xi, who, much like Maimonides did with the Jewish commandments, attempted a reordering of the classical Confucian laws and the establishment of an ethical system that would inform the life of the individual as well as that of society. Both religious thinkers considered the following of the Law an irreplaceable path to the supreme good, and their codifications of legal systems share a philosophical and theological interweaving.[92] Whether this is enough to draw a valid parallel between their philosophies can be debated.

In 1935, Hermann Hesse, whose work the German press had stopped publishing because of the author's pro-Jewish stance, had praised a critical overview of Maimonides' writings by the

Austro-Hungarian scholar Nahum Norbert Glatzer. Two years later, as the Ninth Nazi Party Congress was being held in Nuremberg, Hesse wrote an essay on what he saw as the world's publishing crisis and the fate of the book. Hesse concluded his talk with these words: "Only a few sacred books that humankind treasures hold the regenerating power and survive throughout the millennia and the world crises. It is reassuring to see that the situation does not depend on the distribution of these works. It is not necessary for millions, even hundreds of thousands of readers to have appropriated for themselves this or that sacred book. It is enough that a few people should have been touched by them."[93] Maimonides' books are some of those that touched the happy few.

Conclusion

THE JEWS WERE FIRST expelled from al-Andalus by the Almohads together with their Catholic brethren. Three centuries later, those who had managed to remain were themselves expelled, together with the Arabs this time, by the Catholic kings. At the end of the fifteenth century, Spain conceived of itself as a "clean" society untainted by Jewish or Moorish blood, and tried (unsuccessfully) to impose on the world an identity purified of all Semitic roots. In later years, a reevaluation of these roots, not only in Spain but in the rest of Europe as well, nourished the hope that perhaps the resurgent prejudices of anti-Semitism and Islamophobia might one day be effectively addressed and eventually extinguished, to reach an embracing understanding of a multicultural, multifaceted identity in which reason, not superstition, prevails. It was not to be. In our time, in 2020, in the United States alone, more than 2,100 anti-Semitic incidents were reported, a 12 percent jump and the most in any year since researchers began tracking them four decades earlier.[1] And in Spain, in Maimonides' Sepharad 34.6 percent of the Spanish population (according to a study conducted by Casa Sefarad-Israel in April 2010) expressed an unfavorable opinion of Jews.[2] Much the same is true in most other countries.

In spite of these doleful statistics, the insistence of the Jews on the holiness of the human spirit and the potential of the human mind has not diminished. Caught between the imperialistic greed of certain political powers that claim to represent them (and that would have been abhorrent to the just-minded Maimonides) and the equally abhorrent messianic omens of Orthodox extremists, Jewish identity today still defines itself through a belief in oneness and, for many, a trust in reason. These two need not be contradictory: we can hold, on the one hand, a pervading and essential notion of cosmic integrity, of a coherent and all-pervasive universe for which scientists are still seeking immutable physical laws that might apply to both the macrocosm and the microcosm, and, on the other, the realization that by means of our limited intelligence, we might discover, enunciate, and finally comprehend these laws. We must not lose hope.

Maimonides' life's work can be seen as a heroic effort to restore the golden age of a certain degree of intellectual freedom which, as the years of exile drew on, had become more and more longed-for and remote, and had finally disappeared. Maimonides' greatness lies not in the solutions he may have given to the immemorial questions he raised but in the further questions and fruitful thinking they elicited in his potent mind and in the minds of his readers up to this day, who in their hearts are "always in His presence, while outwardly [they are] with people."[3] Especially, Maimonides believed in placing our trust in the generosity of the Creator who gave his people the sum of all wisdom contained in the Torah.

This absolute trust in God's gift is made explicit in an extraordinary passage in the Talmud: In the midst of a learned discussion, Rabbi Eliezer called on heaven to agree with his own interpretation of Halakhah. In answer to his call, a thunderous voice cried out from above, "Why are you differing with Rabbi Eliezer, as the *halakha* is in accordance with his opinion in every place that he expresses an opinion?" At which Rabbi Joshua arose and quoted Deuteronomy: "It is not in heaven." Longtime after that (but what does time matter in a rabbinical debate?) Rabbi Nathan met the prophet Elijah and asked him about the episode: "What did the Holy One, Blessed be He, do at that time?" Elijah answered, "The Holy One, Blessed be He, smiled and said: My children have triumphed over Me; My children have triumphed over Me."[4]

The experience of faith in the God who gave us reason requires the presence of our will, even when we consider this will a sentiment or discard it as a fictional construct, because the acceptance of an experience (including that of faith) requires that our will guarantee even the *possibility* of having any experience at all. Maimonides fervently believed in the existence of that possibility, however distant. His strong advocacy of reason as the best instrument allotted to the human soul, his natural recourse to the various sources of knowledge available to him, his determination to establish social and personal order in the individual body and in the social one as well, might serve us as a model if we are one day to emerge from the present universal perplexity in the face of so much political, economic, and spiritual turpitude, and begin to lead better, fairer, happier enlightened lives in a (hopefully) not too distant future.

THIS BOOK WAS finished—*besiyata dishmaya*—on 30 March, the probable date of Maimonides' birthday in 1138.

30 March 2021
Lisbon, Portugal

———

Unless otherwise indicated, translations from French, German, Italian, and Spanish are my own. Translations of the Hebrew Bible are from *Tanakh: A New Translation of the Holy Scriptures According to the Traditional Hebrew Text* (Philadelphia: Jewish Publication Society, 1985), with the exception of epigraphs, which are from the King James Version. Qur'an translations are from *The Qur'an: A New Translation*, trans. M. A. S. Abdel Haleem (Oxford: Oxford University Press, 2016), cited by sura. Talmud quotations are from the William Davidson edition, available at Sefaria (sefaria.org). Because different translations can better suit a particular point I am making, I have taken the *Mishneh Torah* quotations from a number of sources, many of which are available at Sefaria; they are identified in the notes by book and section; throughout the text, *Mishneh Torah* book titles follow Sefaria.

Chapter 1. The Figure of Maimonides

1. *Chumash with Targum Onkelos, Haphtaroth and Rashi's Commentary*, 5 vols., trans. A. M. Silbermann in collaboration with

M. Rosenbaum (Jerusalem: Published by the Silbermann Family in arrangement with Routledge & Kegan Paul, [1985]), 2:102–104; Talmud, Bialik 81.

2. Moses Maimonides, *The Guide of the Perplexed*, trans. Shlomo Pines, 2 vols. (Chicago: University of Chicago Press, 1963), Epistle Dedicatory. Since there are several translations of the *Guide*, I have identified quotations by part and chapter number rather than page number.

3. Maimonides, *Mishneh Torah*, Sefer Madda, Repentance 10.6.

4. Salo W. Baron, "The Historical Outlook of Maimonides," in *Proceedings of the American Academy for Jewish Research* 6 (1934–1935): 112.

5. David Yellin and Israel Abrahams, *Maimonides* (Philadelphia: Jewish Publication Society of America, 1903), 217.

6. Leo Strauss, "The Literary Character of *The Guide of the Perplexed*," in Strauss, *Persecution and the Art of Writing* (Glencoe: Free Press, 1952), 74.

7. Walt Whitman, *Song of Myself*, sect. 51.

8. Talmud, Eruvin 54b.

9. Giles Harvey, "Cynthia Ozick's Long Crusade," *New York Times*, 23 June 2016.

10. Maimonides, *Mishneh Torah*, Sefer Madda, Foreign Worship and Customs of the Nations, 2.3.

11. Kenneth Seeskin, "Introduction," in *The Cambridge Companion to Maimonides*, ed. Kenneth Seeskin (Cambridge: Cambridge University Press, 2005), 2.

12. Maimonides, *Guide of the Perplexed*, part III, chapter 4 (hereafter cited as III:4, and so on).

13. Maimonides, *Guide of the Perplexed*, III:12.

14. John Donne, *Sermons* (Berkeley: University of California Press, 1962), 4:102.

Chapter 2. Al-Andalus

1. Nissan Mindel, *The Storyteller*, vol. 5 (Brooklyn, N.Y.: Kehot Publication Society, 1998), 112.

2. Edward Hoffman, *The Wisdom of Maimonides: The Life and Writings of the Jewish Sage* (Boston: Trumpeter Books, 2008), 152.

3. Solomon Zeitlin, *Maimonides: A Biography*, 2nd ed. (New York: Bloch, 1955), 1.

4. Stephen Watson Fullom, *History of William Shakespeare, Player and Poet: With New Facts and Traditions* (London: Saunders, Otley, 1862), 78.

5. Dov Noy, Dan Ben-Amos, and Ellen Frankel, *Folktales of the Jews: Tales from the Sephardic Tradition*, 3 vols. (New York: Jewish Publication Society, 2006), 1:63.

6. Max Meyerhof, "The Medical Works of Maimonides," in *Essays on Maimonides: An Octocentennial Volume*, ed. Salo Wittmayer Baron (New York: Columbia University Press, 1941), 265.

7. See Yitzhack Schwartz, M.D., "The Maimonides Portrait: An Appraisal of One of the World's Most Famous Pictures," *Rambam Maimonides Medical Journal* 2, no. 3 (July 2011): 4–12. A copy of the medallion, created for the U.S. Capitol Building, is pictured in the frontispiece.

8. Various scholars have proposed other dates based on a variety of documents. See Herbert A. Davidson, *Moses Maimonides: The Man and His Works* (Oxford: Oxford University Press, 2005), 6–9.

9. See Charles Verlinden, "Slavery, Slave Trade," in *Dictionary of the Middle Ages*, ed. Joseph R. Strayer, vol. 11 (New York: Scribner's, 1988), 336.

10. Maimonides, *The Guide of the Perplexed*, trans. Shlomo Pines, 2 vols. (Chicago: University of Chicago Press, 1963), III:39.

11. María Rosa Menocal, *The Arabic Role in Medieval Literary History: A Forgotten Heritage* (Philadelphia: University of Pennsylvania Press, 1987), 148. Ella Shohat argues that in the twentieth century, "In the Arab world, 'the Jew' became out of bounds, while in the Jewish state, 'the Arab' became out of bounds; hence, the 'Arab-Jew,' or the 'Jewish-Arab,' inevitably came to seem an ontological impossibility," but that the lost dialogue of cultures could be recaptured if we went "beyond the fait accompli of the violent ruptures, within a reconceived decolonizing framework of mutu-

ally constituted Jewishness and Arabness": Ella Shohat, "The Split Arab/Jew Figure Revisited," *Patterns of Prejudice* 54, nos. 1–2 (2020): 46–70.

12. Quoted in María Rosa Menocal, *The Ornament of the World* (New York: Little, Brown, 2002), 32.

13. Ahmed ibn Mohammed al-Makkari, *The History of the Mohammedan Dynasties in Spain*, trans. Pascual de Gayangos, 2 vols. (London: Routledge Curzon, 2002), 1:30.

14. See S. D. Goitein, *A Mediterranean Society*, rev. and ed. Jacob Lassner (Berkeley: University of California Press, 1999), 233.

15. Peter Cole, *The Dream of the Poem: Hebrew Poetry from Muslim and Christian Spain, 950–1492* (Princeton: Princeton University Press, 2007), 33.

16. Cole, *Dream of the Poem*, 3–4.

17. J.-M. Millás Vallicrosa, "Un capítulo del libro de Poética de Mosé Aben Ezra," *Boletín de la Real Academia Española* 17 (1930): 423–447.

18. *Qur'an*, al-Humaza 104/6–7.

19. Maimonides, *Mishneh Torah*, Sefer Ahavah, Prayer and the Priestly Blessing 1.4.

20. Talmud, Berakhot 28a.

21. al-Makkari, *The History of the Mohammedan Dynasties in Spain*, 1:101.

22. Davidson, *Moses Maimonides*, 13.

23. Ibn Tumart, quoted in Abraham ibn Daud, *The Book of Tradition*, quoted in Davidson, *Moses Maimonides*, 11. Abu Abd Allah Amghar Ibn Tumart was a Muslim Berber religious scholar, teacher, and political leader from the Sous region in southern Morocco.

24. Maimonides, *Epistle to Yemen*, in *Epistles of Maimonides: Crisis and Leadership*, translations and notes by Abraham Halkin, discussions by David Hartman (Philadelphia: Jewish Publication Society, 1985), 15.

25. Isadore Twersky, *Introduction to the Code of Maimonides [Mishneh Torah]* (New Haven: Yale University Press, 1982), 7–9.

Chapter 3. North Africa and Palestine

1. Miguel de Cervantes Saavedra, *Segunda parte del Ingenioso hidalgo don Quijote de la Mancha* (Madrid: Alianza, 1998), 1312.

2. Maimonides, *The Guide of the Perplexed*, trans. Shlomo Pines, 2 vols. (Chicago: University of Chicago Press, 1963), II:9.

3. Ibn Abi Usaybi'a quoted in Herbert A. Davidson, *Moses Maimonides: The Man and His Works* (Oxford: Oxford University Press, 2005), 19; Maimonides, *Epistle on Martyrdom*, in *Epistles of Maimonides: Crisis and Leadership*, translations and notes by Abraham Halkin, discussions by David Hartman (Philadelphia: Jewish Publication Society, 1985), 31.

4. Ammiel Alcalay, *After Jews and Arabs: Remaking Levantine Culture* (Minneapolis: University of Minnesota Press, 1992), 15.

5. Joel L. Kraemer, *Maimonides: The Life and World of One of Civilization's Greatest Minds* (New York: Doubleday, 2008), 59.

6. Quoted in Davidson, *Moses Maimonides*, 30.

7. See Hans Mayer, "Latins, Muslims, and Greeks in the Latin Kingdom of Jerusalem," in *Probleme des lateinischen Königreichs Jerusalem*, Variorum Collected Studies (London: Routledge, 1983), 64; Louis Bréhier, *Histoire anonyme de la première croisade* (Paris: Les Belles Lettres, 1925), 34.

Chapter 4. Egypt

1. Jonathan Phillips, *The Life and Legend of the Sultan Saladin* (New Haven: Yale University Press, 2019), 47.

2. Elisha Russ-Fishbane, *Judaism, Sufism, and the Pietists of Medieval Egypt: A Study of Abraham Maimonides and His Times* (Oxford: Oxford University Press, 2015), 4. This Hasidut is not to be confused with the eighteenth-century branch of Orthodox Judaism founded in Eastern Europe by the Baal Shem Tov.

3. Quoted in Abraham J. Heschel, *Maimonides: The Life and Times of the Great Medieval Jewish Thinker* (New York: Image Books, 1991), 128–129.

4. Aristotle, *Problems*, vol. 1: *Books 1–19*, trans. Robert May-

hew, Loeb Classical Library 316 (Cambridge: Harvard University Press, 2011), 21.

5. See Miguel Ángel González Manjarrés, "La melancolía y lo sobrenatural en la medicina medieval y renacentista," in *Dor, sofrimento e saúde mental na* Arquipatologia *de Filipe Montalto,* ed. Adelino Cardoso and Nuno Miguel Proença (Ribeirão, Portugal: Edições Húmus, 2018), 133.

6. See A. J. Arberry, *The Spiritual Physick of Rhaze* (London: John Murray, 1950), 97.

7. Henry George Farmer, "Maimonides on Listening to Music," *Journal of the Royal Asiatic Society of Great Britain and Ireland* 4 (October 1933): 882.

8. Maimonides, "Letter to Japhet ben Eliahu," in *Letters of Maimonides,* trans. and ed. Leon D. Stitskin (New York: Yeshiva University Press, 1977), 72–73.

9. Maimonides, *The Guide of the Perplexed,* trans. Shlomo Pines, 2 vols. (Chicago: University of Chicago Press, 1963), III:8.

10. Maimonides, *Commentary on the Mishnah,* colophon, in *Introduction to Commentary on Mishnah Avot,* in *A Maimonides Reader,* ed. Isadore Twersky (New York: Behrman House, 1972), 400.

11. Talmud, Nedarim 37a.

12. See Ian Richard Netton, *Al-Farabi and His School* (London: Routledge, London, 1992), 108–109. Among the scholars who doubt the veracity of this story is Joel L. Kraemer, in *Maimonides: The Life and World of One of Civilization's Greatest Minds* (New York: Doubleday, 2008), 161.

13. Md Saifuz Zaman, "The Edification of Sir Walter Scott's Saladin in *The Talisman,*" *Studies in Literature and Language* 1, no. 8 (2010): 39–46.

Chapter 5. Maimonides the Physician

1. Sebastian P. Brock, "Changing Fashions in Syriac Translation Technique: The Background to Syriac Translations Under the Abbasids," *Journal of the Canadian Society for Syriac Studies* 4 (2004): 3–14.

2. See Heinrich Schipperges, *Die Assimilation der arabischen*

Medizin durch das lateinische Mittelalter (Wiesbaden: F. Steiner, 1964).

3. Avicenna, *Avicenna's Medicine: A New Translation of the 11th-Century Canon with Practical Applications for Integrative Health Care*, trans. Mones Abu-Asab, Hakima Amri, and Marc S. Micozzi (Rochester: Healing Arts Press, 2013), 72.

4. Maimonides, *The Eight Chapters of Maimonides on Ethics* (*Shemonah Perakim*): *A Psychological and Ethical Treatise*, trans. Joseph I. Gorfinkle (New York: Columbia University Press, 1912), 35–36.

5. Maimonides, *Mishneh Torah*, Sefer Madda, Human Dispositions 3.2–3.

6. Maimonides, *Mishneh Torah*, Sefer Madda, Foundations of the Torah 4.12.

7. Notably by Bernard Lewis, quoted in Gerrit Bos, "Translator's Introduction to Maimonides," *On Asthma*, trans. Bos (Provo, Utah: Brigham Young University Press, 2002), xxxviii.

8. This is a slightly modified English version of Rashi's commentary on Talmud, Kiddushin 82a, in Adin Steinsaltz, *Koren Talmud Bavli: Kiddushin, Noé Edition* (Jerusalem: Shefa Foundation, 2012), 464n.

9. Quoted in J. O. Leibowitz, "Maimonides on Medical Practice," *Bulletin of the History of Medicine* 31 (1957): 309–317 (310).

10. Maimonides, "Letter to Samuel Ibn Tibbon," in *Letters of Maimonides*, trans. and ed. Leon D. Stitskin (New York: Yeshiva University Press, 1977), 134–135.

11. Quoted in Gerrit Bos, "Maimonides on the Preservation of Health," *Journal of the Royal Asiatic Society*, 3rd ser., 4, no. 2 (July 1994): 230. I have changed the translation a little, according to the German version in H. Kroner, *Der Mediciner Maimonides im Kampfe mit dem Theologen* (Oberdorf-Bopfingen: [Th. Schatzky], 1924). The poem is found in Peter Cole, *The Dream of the Poem: Hebrew Poetry from Muslim and Christian Spain, 950–1492* (Princeton: Princeton University Press, 2007), 24.

12. Maimonides, *Commentary of Hippocrates' Aphorisms*, trans. Gerrit Bos, 2 vols. (Leiden: Koninkijke Brill NV, 2020), 1:222.

13. Maimonides, *Letter on Astrology*, in *A Maimonides Reader*, ed. Isadore Twersky (New York: Behrman House, 1972), 463–473.

14. Maimonides, *On Asthma*, 1.

15. Edward Gibbon, *The History of the Decline and Fall of the Roman Empire*, ed. J. B. Bury (New York: Heritage, 1946), 1:138.

16. Maimonides, *On Asthma*, 55.

Chapter 6. Maimonides the Scholar

1. Abraham S. Halkin, "The Judeo-Islamic Age," in *Great Ages and Ideas of the Jewish People*, ed. Leo W. Schwarz (New York: Modern Library, 1956), 220. See also Norman Roth, "Maimonides on Hebrew Language and Poetry," *Hebrew Studies* 26, no. 1 (1985): 93–101.

2. Maimonides, "Letter to Samuel Ibn Tibbon," in *Letters of Maimonides*, trans. and ed. Leon D. Stitskin (New York: Yeshiva University Press, 1977), 133.

3. See Norman Roth, "Maimonides on Hebrew Language and Poetry," *Hebrew Studies* 26, no. 1's introduction to Maimonides, *Dux neutrorum vel dubiorum*, Part I, ed. Diana Di Segni (Leuven: Peeters, 2019), 13.

4. Rabbi Joseph B. Soloveitchik has found in these strategies a "lack of creativity": "His subjective approach to God was unique but his arguments were traditional and resembled those of Thomas Aquinas and Albertus Magnus." Rabbi Joseph B. Soloveitchik, *Maimonides: Between Philosophy and Halakah*, ed. Lawrence J. Kaplan (Jerusalem: KTAV, 2016), 76.

5. Maimonides, *The Guide of the Perplexed*, trans. Shlomo Pines, 2 vols. (Chicago: University of Chicago Press, 1963), I:59; the quotation is from Dante: "A l'alta fantasia qui mancò possa" (*Paradiso*, 33.142).

6. *The Mishnah*, trans. Herbert Danby (Oxford: Oxford University Press, 1933; 1989), 449.

7. Menahem Ben-Sasson, "The Maimonidean Dynasty," in *Maimonides After 800 Years: Essays on Maimonides and His Influence*, ed. Jay M. Harris (Cambridge: Harvard University Press, 2007), 7.

8. Seneca, "Epistle XLIV," in *Epistles*, vol. 1: *Epistles 1–65*, trans. Richard M. Gummere, Loeb Classical Library 75 (Cambridge: Harvard University Press, 1917), 289.

Chapter 7. Maimonides the Philosopher

1. See David Daube, "Rabbinic Methods of Interpretation and Hellenistic Rhetoric," *Hebrew Union College Annual* 22 (1949): 239–264.

2. Titus Flavius Josephus, *Against Apion*, in *The Complete Works of Josephus in Ten Volumes*, a new and revised edition based on Havercamp's translation (Cleveland: World Syndicate Publishing, n.d.), 10:442.

3. William Smith, ed., *Dictionary of Greek and Roman Biography and Mythology*, 3 vols. (Boston: Little, Brown, 1849), 1:781.

4. Johannes Pedersen, *The Arabic Book*, trans. Geoffrey French (Princeton: Princeton University Press, 1984), 106.

5. Quoted in Robert Van der Weyer, *366 Readings from Islam* (Mumbai: Jaico, 2000), 21.

6. A. Badawi, *La transmission de la philosophie grecque au monde arabe* (Paris: Vrin, 1968), 56.

7. Averroes (Ibn Rushd) of Cordoba, *Long Commentary on the De Anima of Aristotle*, trans. Richard C. Taylor with Thérèse-Anne Druart (New Haven: Yale University Press, 2009), 1.

8. Aristotle, *De interpretatione* 19a23–19a24, in Aristotle, *Categories and De Interpretatione*, trans. J. L. Ackrill (Oxford: Clarendon Aristotle Series, 1966), 52.

9. Philo of Alexandria, *On the Embassy to Gaius*, I, quoted in Maren R. Niehoff, *Philo of Alexandria: An Intellectual Biography* (New Haven: Yale University Press, 2018), 26.

10. Demosthenes, *Third Olynthiac*, in *Orations*, vol. 1: *Orations 1–17, 20; Olynthiacs, Philippics, Minor Public Orations*, trans. J. H. Vince, Loeb Classical Library 238 (Cambridge: Harvard University Press, 1930), 53.

11. Hermann Cohen, *Der Begriff der Religion im System der Philosophie* (Giessen: De Gruyter, 1915), 13.

12. Aristotle, *Nicomachean Ethics*, trans. H. Rackham, rev. ed., 10.7.1177b, Loeb Classical Library 73 (Cambridge: Harvard University Press, 1934), 617.

13. Pierre Bouretz, *Lumières du Moyen Age: Maïmonide philosophe* (Paris: Gallimard, 2015), 898.

14. Quoted in Marc Saperstein, *Jewish Preaching, 1200–1800: An Anthology* (New Haven: Yale University Press, 1989), 378–379.

15. Bouretz, *Lumières du Moyen Age*, 452.

16. Leo Strauss, *Philosophy and Law: Contributions to the Understanding of Maimonides and His Predecessors*, trans. Eve Adler (Albany: State University of New York Press, 1995), 72.

17. See Jean-Pierre Vernant, *Les origines de la pensée grec* (Paris: PUF, 1962), 85.

18. As Eve Krakowski notes, "In the spring of 1176, Maimonides ordered Jewish women throughout Egypt to observe rabbinic menstrual purity laws or risk major financial loss: the dowers their husbands had promised them at marriage. Scholars have understood this decree mainly in context of Karaite-Rabbanite relations, or as inspired by a mass refusal among women in twelfth-century Egypt to perform rabbinic immersion. Both frameworks were first suggested by Maimonides himself, but both are misleading." Maimonides' decree might have instead responded to an otherwise unknown aspect of medieval "common Judaism": a quasi-biblical and nonrabbinic—but not markedly Karaite—menstrual purity regime "that had prevailed among Jews throughout the medieval Middle East for centuries": Eve Krakowski, "Maimonides' Menstrual Reform in Egypt," *Jewish Quarterly Review* 110, no. 2 (Spring 2020): 245–289 (245).

19. Maimonides, "Letter to Samuel Ibn Tibbon," in *Letters of Maimonides*, trans. and ed. Leon D. Stitskin (New York: Yeshiva University Press, 1977), 135.

20. Maimonides, *The Eight Chapters of Maimonides on Ethics (Shemonah Peraḳim): A Psychological and Ethical Treatise*, trans. Joseph I. Gorfinkle (New York: Columbia University Press, 1912), 35–36.

21. Joel L. Kraemer, *Maimonides: The Life and World of One of Civilization's Greatest Minds* (New York: Doubleday, 2008), 18.

22. Plato, *Republic* 5.476d, trans. Paul Shorey, in *The Collected Dialogues*, ed. Edith Hamilton and Huntington Cairns, 2nd ed. (Princeton: Princeton University Press, 1963), 716. Aristotle disagrees with Plato and speaks of *phantasia: De Anima* 3.3, trans. Hugh Lawson-Tancred (London: Penguin, 2015), 109.

23. Samuel Taylor Coleridge, remark made on 2 July 1830 and recorded by Henry Nelson Coleridge in *Table Talk*, Part I [1835] in *The Collected Works of Samuel Taylor Coleridge*, ed. Carl Woodring, 16 vols. (Princeton: Princeton University Press, 1990), 14:172.

24. Seneca, "Epistle XLI" in *Epistles*, vol. 1: *Epistles 1–65*, trans. Richard M. Gummere, Loeb Classical Library 75 (Cambridge: Harvard University Press, 1917), 273.

25. Maimonides, *The Guide of the Perplexed*, trans. Shlomo Pines, 2 vols. (Chicago: University of Chicago Press, 1963), Introduction to the First Part.

26. Rabbi Ya'akov Mosheh Harlap, quoted in Marvin Fox, "The Doctrine of the Mean in Aristotle and Maimonides," in *Collected Essays on Philosophy and on Judaism*, ed. Jacob Neusner, 3 vols., Academic Studies in the History of Judaism (Binghamton, N.Y.: Global Publications, 2001), 1:42.

27. Immanuel Kant, *Metaphysical Principles of Virtue*, Part 2 of *The Metaphysics of Morals*, trans. James W. Ellington (Indianapolis: Bobbs-Merrill, 1968), 95.

28. Babylonian Talmud, Menahot 29b, quoted in Yosef Hayim Yerushalmi, *Zakhor: Jewish History and Jewish Memory* (Seattle: University of Washington Press, 1989), 19.

29. Jack Miles, *God, A Biography* (New York: Knopf, 1995), 16.

30. Babylonian Talmud, Avodah Zarah 3b.

31. William Tyndale, "Prologue to the Prophet Jonas," section 8, in *Doctrined Treatises and Introductions to Different Portions of the Holy Scriptures* (Oxford: Parker Society, 1848), 449.

32. Saadia Gaon, *The Book of Beliefs and Opinions*, trans. Samuel Rosenblatt (New Haven: Yale University Press, 1942), 56.

33. *Aristotle: Metaphysics*, vol. 1: *Books 1–9*, trans. Hugh Tredennick, 2.1.993a–b, Loeb Classical Library 271 (Cambridge: Harvard University Press, 1933), 85.

34. Philo of Alexandria, *On the Migration of Abraham* 13, quoted in Niehoff, *Philo of Alexandria*, 182.

35. Maimonides, *Guide of the Perplexed*, III:13.

36. Averroes (Ibn Rushd) of Cordoba, *Long Commentary*, xv.

Chapter 8. Maimonides the Believer

1. Maimonides, "Ma'amar Hayichud or Treatise on the Unity of God," in *The Existence and Unity of God: Three Treatises Attributed to Moses Maimonides*, trans. Fred Rosner (Northvale, N.J.: Jason Aronson, 1990), 46.

2. Aristotle, *Metaphysics*, vol. 1: *Books 1–9*; vol. 2: *Books 10–14*, trans. Hugh Tredennick, 1.5.986b, 12.7.1072b, Loeb Classical Library 271, 287 (Cambridge: Harvard University Press, 1933, 1935), 39, 151.

3. Quoted in "Philo Judæus," in *The Jewish Encyclopedia*, 12 vols., ed. Isidore Singer (New York: Funk & Wagnalls, 1901–1906), 10:11.

4. Maimonides, *Mishneh Torah*, Sefer Madda, Foundations of the Torah 1.1, 1.7.

5. Maimonides, *Mishneh Torah*, Sefer Madda, Foundations of the Torah 1.12.

6. Marvin Fox, "The Doctrine of the Mean in Aristotle and Maimonides," in *Collected Essays on Philosophy and on Judaism*, ed. Jacob Neusner, 3 vols., Academic Studies in the History of Judaism (Binghamton, N.Y.: Global Publications, 2001), 1:62.

7. See Miira Tuominen, *The Ancient Commentators on Plato and Aristotle* (Los Angeles: University of California Press, 2009), 237.

8. Maimonides, *Guide of the Perplexed*, I:50.

9. See Daniel J. Lasker, "Tradition and Innovation in Maimonides' Attitude Toward Other Religions," in *Maimonides after 800 Years: Essays on Maimonides and His Influence*, ed. Jay M. Harris (Cambridge: Harvard University Press, 2007), 167.

10. David Novak, *Maimonides' View of Christianity*, Oxford Scholarship Online (1992), October 2011, 59: DOI:10.1093/acprof :oso/9780195072730.003.0004.

11. Maimonides, *Guide of the Perplexed*, I:31 (Maimonides repeats this quotation in his *Treatise on Asthma*).

12. Aristotle, *De Anima*, 2.414a, trans. Christopher Shields (Oxford: Clarendon, 2016), 26.

13. Maimonides, *The Eight Chapters of Maimonides on Ethics*, 201.

14. Solomon ibn Gabirol, *The Fountain of Life*, trans. Harry E. Wedeck (New York: Philosophical Library, 1962), 42.

15. See "Solomon ben Luria," in *The Jewish Encyclopedia*, 8:210.

Chapter 9. How Should One Live?

1. Maimonides, *Iggeret ha-Shemad* or *Maamar Kiddush ha-Shem*, in *Letters of Maimonides*, trans. and ed. Leon D. Stitskin (New York: Yeshiva University Press, 1977), 63.

2. Maimonides, *Iggeret ha-Shemad*, 40–41.

3. Maimonides, *Iggeret ha-Shemad*, 43.

4. Maimonides, *Iggeret ha-Shemad*, 65.

5. Haggai Mazuz, "The Identity of the Apostate in the Epistle to Yemen," *AJS Review* 38, no. 2 (November 2014): 363–374.

6. Maimonides, *Epistle to Yemen*, in *Epistles of Maimonides: Crisis and Leadership*, translations and notes by Abraham Halkin, discussions by David Hartman (Philadelphia: Jewish Publication Society, 1985), 95.

7. Maimonides, *Epistle to Yemen*, 95.

8. Maimonides, *Epistle to Yemen*, 111–113.

9. Babylonian Talmud, Yoma 9b.

Chapter 10. Lessons from Exodus

1. Quoted in William C. Chittick, *The Self-Disclosure of God: Principles of Ibn al-'Arabi's Cosmology* (New York: State University of New York Press, 1998), 20–21.

2. Maimonides, *The Guide of the Perplexed*, trans. Shlomo Pines, 2 vols. (Chicago: University of Chicago Press, 1963), I:2.

3. Maimonides, *Guide of the Perplexed*, III:29.

4. See Salo W. Baron, "The Historical Outlook of Maimonides," *Proceedings of the American Academy for Jewish Research* 6 (1934–1935): 7.

5. Maimonides, *Introduction to the Commentary on Mishnah Avot*, in *A Maimonides Reader*, ed. Isadore Twersky (New York: Behrman House, 1972), 365.

6. Maimonides, *Guide of the Perplexed*, I:70.

7. Maimonides, *Guide of the Perplexed*, III:22.

8. Moshe Halbertal, *Maimonides: Life and Thought* (Princeton: Princeton University Press, 2014), 162.

9. This is the ninth of Maimonides' thirteen principles. See Aryeh Kaplan, *Maimonides' Principles: The Fundamentals of Jewish Faith* (New York: National Conference of Synagogue Youth, 1975).

Chapter 11 . The Talmud

1. Adin Steinsaltz, *The Essential Talmud*, trans. Chaya Galai (New York: Basic, 1976), 3.

2. Steinsaltz, *The Essential Talmud*, 7.

3. Steinsaltz, *The Essential Talmud*, 9.

4. Maimonides, *Introduction to the Talmud: A Translation of the Rambam's Introduction to His Commentary on the Mishnah*, trans. Zvi Lampel (Brooklyn, N.Y.: Judaica, 1998), 182.

5. Heinrich Gaetz, *Geschichte der Juden*, vol. 5: *Vom Aufblüßen der Jüdisch-Spanischen Kultur (1027) bis Maimuni's Tod (1205)* (Leipzig: Oscar Leiner, 1895), 293–294.

Chapter 12. The Law

1. See Raphael Jospe, "The Book of Job as a Biblical Guide of the Perplexed," in *Jewish Philosophy: Foundations and Extensions*, vol. 2: *On Philosophers and Their Thought* (Lanham, Md.: University Press of America, 2008), 97–106.

2. Yosef Hayim Yerushalmi, *The Lisbon Massacre of 1506 and the Royal Image in the "Shebet Yehudah,"* Hebrew Union College Annual Supplements 1 (Cincinnati: Hebrew Union College Press, 1976), xi.

3. Fred Rosner, *The Existence and Unity of God: Three Treatises Attributed to Moses Maimonides* (Northvale, N.J.: Jason Aronson, 1990), 207.

4. George Steiner, *In Bluebeard's Castle: Some Notes Towards the Redefinition of Culture* (New Haven: Yale University Press, 1971), 76.

5. Steiner, *In Bluebeard's Castle*, 37, 41.

6. Note that whereas the JPS *Tanakh* uses the singular "god," the KJV has "gods": "These be thy gods, O Israel, which brought thee up out of the land of Egypt" (Exodus 4).

7. Aryeh Kaplan, *Maimonides' Principles: The Fundamentals of Jewish Faith* (New York: National Conference of Synagogue Youth, 1975), 6.

8. Kaplan, *Maimonides' Principles*, 8.

9. Maimonides, *The Guide of the Perplexed*, trans. Shlomo Pines, 2 vols. (Chicago: University of Chicago Press, 1963), III:22.

10. Étienne Gilson, "Homage to Maimonides," in *Essays on Maimonides: An Octocentennial Volume*, ed. Salo Wittmayer Baron (New York: Columbia University Press, 1941), 21.

11. *Maimonides' Commentary on the Mishnah—Tractate Sanhedrin*, trans. Fred Rosner (New York: Sepher-Hermon Press, 1981), 157.

12. Kaplan, *Maimonides' Principles*, 8.

13. Maimonides, *The Eight Chapters of Maimonides on Ethics (Shemonah Peraḳim): A Psychological and Ethical Treatise*, trans. Joseph I. Gorfinkle (New York: Columbia University Press, 1912), 361.

14. Alfred L. Ivry, *Maimonides' "Guide of the Perplexed": A Philosophical Guide* (Chicago: University of Chicago Press, 2016), 27.

15. Zohar 2:98b, quoted in Elliot Wolfson, *Through a Speculum That Shines: Vision and Imagination in Medieval Jewish Mysticism* (Princeton: Princeton University Press, 1994).

16. Marc B. Shapiro, *Studies in Maimonides and His Interpreters* (Scranton, Pa.: University of Scranton Press, 2008), 85–93.

17. Heinrich Graetz, "Die Konstruktion der jüdischen Geschichte," *Zeitschrift für die religiösen Interessen des Judentums*, 11 (1846): 416.

18. *Genesis Rabbah* 51, quoted in Maimonides, *Guide of the Perplexed*, III:10. (*Genesis Rabbah* is a midrashic text from between 300 and 500 CE.)

19. Aristotle, *Physics*, vol. 1: *Books 1–4*, trans. P. H. Wicksteed and F. M. Cornford, 1.7.190a13–1.7.191a22, Loeb Classical Library 228 (Cambridge: Harvard University Press, 1957), 77–80.

20. Maimonides, *Guide of the Perplexed*, III:8; III:10.

21. Maimonides, *Guide of the Perplexed*, III:23.

22. Maimonides, *Guide of the Perplexed*, III:20.

23. Quoted in Yosef Hayim Yerushalmi, *Zakhor: Jewish History and Jewish Memory* (Seattle: University of Washington Press, 1989), 124.

24. A. Berger, "Captive at the Gate of Rome: The Story of a Messianic Motif," *Proceedings of the American Academy for Jewish Research* 44 (1977): 1–17 (12).

Chapter 13. The *Mishneh Torah*

1. Maimonides, *The Eight Chapters of Maimonides on Ethics* (*Shemonah Peraķim*): *A Psychological and Ethical Treatise*, trans. Joseph I. Gorfinkle (New York: Columbia University Press, 1912), 54–55.

2. See Marc B. Shapiro, *Studies in Maimonides and His Interpreters* (Scranton, Pa.: University of Scranton Press, 2008), 2.

3. Simone Weil, *The Notebooks of Simone Weil*, trans. Arthur Willis (London: Routledge and Kegan Paul, 1956), 421.

4. Maimonides, *The Guide of the Perplexed*, trans. Michael Friedländer (New York: Cosimo Classics, 2007), III:32.

5. Maimonides, *The Guide of the Perplexed*, trans. Shlomo Pines, 2 vols. (Chicago: University of Chicago Press, 1963), III:28.

6. Talmud Bavli, Berachot 4a.

7. Avicenna, "Predestination," in *Avicenna on Theology*, trans. A. J. Arberry (Dubai: Kitab al-Islamiyyah, n/d) 41.

8. Isadore Twersky, *Introduction to the Code of Maimonides* (*Mishneh Torah*) (New Haven: Yale University Press, 1980), 97.

9. Maimonides, *Mishneh Torah*, Introduction: Transmission of the Oral Law 42.

10. This translation is from the JPS *Tanakh* of 1917; the term "mighty hand" also appeared in the King James Version. The 1985 edition has "And for all the great might and awesome power that Moses displayed before all Israel."

11. Jorge Luis Borges, "Las versiones homéricas," in *Discusión* (Buenos Aires: Manuel Gleizer, 1932), 44.

12. See Aryeh Kaplan, *Maimonides' Principles: The Fundamentals of Jewish Faith* (New York: National Conference of Synagogue Youth, 1975), 5.

13. Quoted in *Iggerot HaRambam*, ed. Yitzhak Shilat (Jerusalem: Birkat Moshe, 1988), 390.

14. See Raymond L. Weiss, "Some Notes on Twersky's *Introduction to the Code of Maimonides*," *Jewish Quarterly Review* n.s., 74, no. 1 (July, 1983): 61–79.

15. See *Epistles of Maimonides: Crisis and Leadership*, translations and notes by Abraham Halkin, discussions by David Hartman (Philadelphia: Jewish Publication Society, 1985), ix.

16. Adina Hoffman and Peter Cole, *Sacred Trash: The Lost and Found World of the Cairo Geniza* (New York: Schocken, 2011).

17. Maimonides, *Mishneh Torah*, Sefer Zemanim, Leavened and Unleavened Bread, 7.12.

18. Stendhal, *Lettre à M. de Balzac*, 30 October 1840, in *Correspondance*, 3 vols. (1800–1842) (Paris: C. Bosse, 1908), 2:108.

19. Maimonides, *Mishneh Torah*, Sefer Madda, Foundations of the Torah 4.13.

Chapter 14. *The Guide of the Perplexed*

1. Shlomo Pines, "Translator's Introduction," in Maimonides, *The Guide of the Perplexed*, trans. Shlomo Pines, 2 vols. (Chicago: University of Chicago Press, 1963) lxxix.

2. Maimonides, *Guide of the Perplexed*, I:Introduction.

3. Quoted in Ibn Tufayl, *Hayy ibn Yaqzan: A Philosophical Tale*, trans. Len Evan Goodman (New York: Twayne, 1972), 138.

4. Maimonides, *Guide of the Perplexed*, I:Introduction.

5. Shelomo Dov Goitein, quoted in Warren Zev Harvey, "A Guide of the Perplexed," Tablet Online Magazine, January 8, 2021

(https://www.tabletmag.com/sections/history/articles/goitein
-maimonides-guide-of-the-perplexed).

6. Maimonides, *Guide of the Perplexed*, II:32.

7. Joshua Parens, *Maimonides and Spinoza: Their Conflicting Views of Human Nature* (Chicago: University of Chicago Press, 2012), 179–180.

8. See Moshe Halbertal, *Maimonides: Life and Thought*, trans. Joel Linsider (Princeton: Princeton University Press, 2014), 7.

9. Maimonides, *Guide of the Perplexed*, I:Introduction.

10. Quoted in Rabbi Ben Zion Bokser, *The Wisdom of the Talmud: A Thousand Years of Jewish Thought* (New York: Citadel, 1951), 90.

11. Heinrich Graetz, *Geschichte der Juden*, vol. 5 (Leipzig: Oskar Leiner, 1882), 293–294.

12. In the *Commedia* (*Paradiso* 4.43–48) Beatrice explains as much to Dante:

> Per questo la Scrittura condescende
> a vostra facultate, e piedi e mano
> attribuisce a Dio e altro intende;
>
> e Santa Chiesa con aspetto umano
> Gabrïel e Michel vi rappresenta,
> e l'altro che Tobia rifece sano.
>
> [That is why Scripture condescends
> To your capability and attributes to God
> Hands and feet, meaning something different;
>
> and Holy Church depicts for you
> Gabriel and Michael with human aspect,
> And that other one who healed Tobit.]

13. Quoted by Roger Pearse, "Thoughts on Antiquity, Patristics, Information Access, and More," Galen, https://www.roger
-pearse.com/weblog/tag/galen/.

14. Aryeh Kaplan, *Maimonides' Principles: The Fundamentals of Jewish Faith* (New York: National Conference of Synagogue Youth, 1975), 8.

15. Maimonides, *Essay on Resurrection*, in *Epistles of Maimonides: Crisis and Leadership*, translations and notes by Abraham Halkin, discussions by David Hartman (Philadelphia: Jewish Publication Society, 1985), 211.

16. Maimonides, *Essay on Resurrection*, 210. On the controversy surrounding the authenticity of this essay, see Albert D. Friedberg, "Maimonides' Reinterpretation of the Thirteenth Article of Faith: Another Look at the Essay on Resurrection," *Jewish Studies Quarterly* 10 (2003): 244–257.

17. Maimonides, *Essay on Resurrection*, 221.

18. Quoted in Kalman P. Bland, *The Artless Jew: Medieval and Modern Affirmations and Denials of the Visual* (Princeton: Princeton University Press, 2000), 81.

19. See Sarah Stroumsa, "The Elegance of Precision," in *Maimonides' "Guide of the Perplexed" in Translation: A History from the Thirteenth Century to the Twentieth*, ed. Joseph Stern, James T. Robinson, and Yonatan Shemesh (Chicago: University of Chicago Press, 2019), 235.

20. Maimonides, *Essay on Resurrection*, 221.

21. *Aristotle: Metaphysics*, vol. 1: *Books 1–9*, trans. Hugh Tredennick, 1.982b, Loeb Classical Library 271 (Cambridge: Harvard University Press, 1933), 13

22. See Chana Heilbrun, "Coleridge and Judaism," *Immanuel* 21 (Summer 1987): 111–114; Maimonides, *Guide of the Perplexed*, I:2.

23. Coleridge quoted in Heilbrun, "Coleridge and Judaism," 113.

24. Samuel Taylor Coleridge, "Lecture X: Donne, Dante, Milton, *Paradise Lost*," in *The Complete Works of Samuel Taylor Coleridge*, vol. 4, ed. Professor [William G. T.] Shedd (New York: Harper, 1853), 290. The same idea appears earlier in Dante's *Commedia* (*Paradiso* 4.40–42) when Beatrice says to Dante:.

Così parlar conviensi al vostro ingenio,
però che solo da sensato apprende
ciò che fa poseia d'intelleto degno.

[This manner of speaking suits your intelligence

Since only through the sense of perception you can learn
That which will become fit for your intellect.]

25. See Sarah Stroumsa, *Maimonides in His World: Portrait of a Mediterranean Thinker* (Princeton: Princeton University Press, 2009), 3–7.

26. Maimonides, "Letter to the Jews of Marseilles," in *Letters of Maimonides*, trans. and ed. Leon D. Stitskin (New York: Yeshiva University Press, 1977), 119.

27. Samuel Taylor Coleridge, "The Friend," in *The Collected Works of Samuel Taylor Coleridge*, vol. 4, ed. Barbara E. Rooke (Princeton: Princeton University Press, 1969), 97.

28. Maimonides, *Guide of the Perplexed*, III:51.

29. Maimonides, *Guide of the Perplexed*, III:51.

30. Kaplan, *Maimonides' Principles*, 8.

31. Maimonides, *The Guide of the Perplexed*, II:51. Maimonides interprets the verse from the Song of Solomon 5:2 as referring to true prophecy, and purposely excludes divination: "I sleep, but my heart waketh; / Hark! my beloved knocketh."

32. Maimonides, *Guide of the Perplexed*, I:Introduction.

33. Maimonides, *Guide of the Perplexed*, III:Introduction.

34. Jerusalem Talmud, Chagigah 77C, in *Midrash Rabbah: Genesis*, trans. H. Freedman and Maurice Simon, vols. 1–2 (London: Soncino Press, 1983).

35. Maimonides, *Guide of the Perplexed*, I:Introduction.

36. Leo Strauss, *Persecution and the Art of Writing* (Chicago: University of Chicago Press, 1952) 55.

37. See Herbert A. Davidson, *Moses Maimonides: The Man and His Works* (Oxford: Oxford University Press, 2005), 178–179.

Chapter 15. What Is Virtue?

1. See Joshua Parens, *Maimonides and Spinoza: Their Conflicting Views of Human Nature* (Chicago: University of Chicago Press, 2012), 20.

2. See Amos Funkenstein, *Maimonides: Nature, History and Messianic Belief* (Woodstock, Vt.: Jewish Lights, 1998), 59.

3. R. Yitzchak Blau, "Is Courage a Jewish Value?" *Tradition: A Journal of Orthodox Jewish Thought* 42, no. 4 (Winter 2009): 33–49 (34).

4. *The Babylonian Talmud: Sanhedrin*, trans. Jacob Shachter (chaps. 1–6) and H. Freedman (chap. 7) (London: Soncino, 1935), chap. 2.

5. See Han Baltussen, "Plato *Protagoras* 340–348: Commentary in the Making?" *Bulletin of the Institute of Classical Studies*, supplement 83 (2004): 21–35.

6. Plato, *Protagoras* 320c–323a, trans. W. K. C. Guthrie, in *The Collected Dialogues of Plato Including the Letters*, ed. Edith Hamilton and Huntington Cairns (Princeton: Princeton University Press, 1963), 318–320.

7. Leo Strauss compares Al-Farabi's utopian idea with a concept put forward by Maimonides in the *Guide* (III:34 and II:40) of laws born out of a specific conflict from opposing opinions at different times. Leo Strauss, "Quelques remarques sur la Science politique de Maïmonide et de Farabi," *Revue des études juives* 100 bis, nos. 199–200 (1936): 1–37.

8. Plato, *Republic* 5.473d–e, trans. Paul Shorey, in *The Collected Dialogues of Plato*, 712.

9. Maimonides, *The Eight Chapters of Maimonides on Ethics (Shemonah Perakim): A Psychological and Ethical Treatise*, trans. Joseph I. Gorfinkle (New York: Columbia University Press, 1912), 265.

10. Maimonides, *Mishneh Torah*, Sefer Shoftim, Kings and Wars 11–12, quoted in Gershom Scholem, "Toward an Understanding of the Messianic Idea in Judaism," trans. Michael A. Meyer, in *The Messianic Idea in Judaism: and Other Essays on Jewish Spirituality* (New York: Schocken, 1971), 28.

11. Sabato Morais, "A Letter by Maimonides to the Jews of South Arabia Entitled 'The Inspired Hope,'" *Jewish Quarterly Review* 25, no. 4 (1935): 330–369 (333).

12. Scholem, "Toward an Understanding of the Messianic Idea in Judaism," 25.

13. Aryeh Kaplan, *Maimonides' Principles: The Fundamentals of*

Jewish Faith (New York: National Conference of Synagogue Youth, 1975), 8; Maimonides, *The Guide of the Perplexed*, trans. Shlomo Pines, 2 vols. (Chicago: University of Chicago Press, 1963), I:Introduction.

Chapter 16. Reading Maimonides

1. Lewis Carroll, *Through the Looking-Glass* (1896), in *The Annotated Alice*, ed. Martin Gardner (New York: Clarkson Potter, 1960), 219.

2. Maimonides, *The Guide of the Perplexed*, trans. Shlomo Pines, 2 vols. (Chicago: University of Chicago Press, 1963), I:Introduction.

3. Isadore Twersky, *Introduction to the Code of Maimonides* (New Haven: Yale University Press, 1982), 520.

4. See Herbert A. Davidson, *Moses Maimonides: The Man and His Works* (Oxford: Oxford University Press, 2005) 297.

5. Mayer Kayserling, "Adret, Solomon ben Abraham," in *The Jewish Encyclopedia* (New York: Funk and Wagnalls, 1905), 1:212; Raphael Jospe and Dov Schwartz, "Maimonidean Controversy," *Encyclopedia Judaica* (2008), available at Jewish Virtual Library, https://www.jewishvirtuallibrary.org/maimonidean-controversy.

6. See Allan Nadler, "The 'Rambam Revival' in Early Modern Jewish Thought: Maskilim, Mitnagdim, and Hasidim on Maimondes' Guide of the Perplexed," in *Maimonides After 800 Years: Essays on Maimonides and His Influence*, ed. Jay Michael Harris (Cambridge: Harvard University Press, 2007), 37.

7. See Isaac E. Barzilay, *Between Reason and Faith: Anti-Rationalism in Italian Jewish Thought, 1250–1650* (The Hague: Mouton, 1967), 25.

8. Quoted in Jay Harris, "The Image of Maimonides in Nineteenth-Century Jewish Historiography," *Proceedings of the American Society for Jewish Research* 54 (1987): 119.

9. Nadler, "The 'Rambam Revival' in Early Modern Jewish Thought," 49.

10. Quoted in Nadler, "The 'Rambam Revival' in Early Modern Jewish Thought," 55.

11. James T. Robinson, *Samuel Ibn Tibbon's Commentary on Ecclesiastes: The Book of the Soul of Man* (Tübingen: Mohr Siebeck, 2007), para. 35.

12. Aristotle, *Nicomachean Ethics*, trans. H. Rackham, 1.14, Loeb Classical Library 73 (Cambridge: Harvard University Press, 1926), 33.

13. Igor H. De Souza, *Rewriting Maimonides: Early Commentaries on the "Guide of the Perplexed"* (Berlin: De Gruyter, 2018), 2.

14. Dante, *Inferno*, 20.116–117: "Michele Scotto fu, che veramente / de le magiche frode seppe 'l gioco."

15. Quoted in Ernest Renan, *Qu'est-ce qu'une nation?* (Paris: Flammarion, 2011), 320–322.

16. Eric Lawee, *Isaac Abarbanel's Stance Toward Tradition: Defense, Dissent, and Dialogue* (Albany: State University of New York Press, 2001), 74–75.

17. Nathan Hofer, "Abraham Abulafia's 'Mystical' Reading of the 'Guide for the Perplexed,'" *Numen* 60, nos. 2/3 (2013), 217–218.

18. See Cyril Aslanov, "L'aristotelisme mediéval au service du commentaire litéral: le cas de Joseph Caspi," *Revue d'études juifs* 161, no. 1 (2002), 123–137.

19. Quoted in Barzilay, *Between Reason and Faith*, 91.

20. Quoted in Barzilay, *Between Reason and Faith*, 91.

21. See Isaac E. Barzilay, *Between Reason and Faith*, 127.

22. Quoted in Lawee, *Isaac Abarbanel's Stance Toward Tradition*, 54.

23. Jacobus de Voragine, *The Golden Legend: Readings on the Saints*, trans. William Granger Ryan (Princeton: Princeton University Press, 2012).

24. See Gregor Schwarb, "The Reception of Maimonides in Christian-Arabic Literature," in *Ben 'Ever la-'Arav: Maimonides and His World: Contacts Between Arabic Literature and Jewish Literature in the Middle Ages and Modern Times*, ed. Y. Tobi (Haifa: University of Haifa Press, 2014), 140.

25. Dante, *Commedia, Purgatorio* 8.37–39; *Inferno* 9.76.

26. See Giuseppe Sermoneta, "La fantasia e l'attività fantastica nella scuola filosofica del Maimonide," in *Phantasia-imaginatio:*

Colloquio internazionale Lessico Intellettuale europeo, Rome, 9–11 January 1986. Atti a cura di M. Fattori e M. Bianchi (Rome: Ateneo, 1988).

27. See G. Blustein, *Storia degli ebrei in Roma dal 140 av. Cr. fino ad oggi* (Rome: P. Maglione & C. Strini, 1921), 73–80.

28. Guy Shaked, *Immanuel the Roman's Critique of Dante's "Divine Comedy" and Maimonides' "Guide for the Perplexed"* (Printed in Great Britain by Amazon), 6.

29. See J. Goldenthal, *Il Dante Ebreo ossia il Picciol santuario, poema didattico in terza rima, di Mosé da Rieti . . . per la prima volta pubblicato dal dott. Jacob Goldenthal* (Vienna: n.p. 1851).

30. Étienne Gilson, *Dante the Philosopher* (New York: Sheed and Ward, 1949), 179.

31. Maimonides, *Guide of the Perplexed*, I:58.

32. Émile Saisset, "La Philosophie des Juifs: Maïmonide et Spinoza," *Revue des Deux Mondes* 37 (1862): 296–325.

33. Thomas Aquinas, *Summa Theologica*, 13:a, trans. Fathers of the English Dominican Province (New York: Benzinger, 1947), 1:61.

34. Thomas Aquinas, "Commentary on the *De Trinitate* of Boethiius," quoted in Isaac Franck, "Maimonides and Aquinas on Man's Knowledge of God: A Twentieth Century Perspective," *Review of Metaphysics* 38, no. 3 (March 1985): 591–615.

35. See Jacob I. Dienstag, "Maimonides in English Christian Thought and Scholarship: An Alphabetical Survey," *Hebrew Studies* 26, no. 2 (1985): 249–299.

36. See S. Harrison Thomson, *The Writings of Robert Grosseteste* (Cambridge: Cambridge University Press, 1940), 265.

37. See Jeremiah Hackett, "Maimonides and Bacon: Did Roger Bacon Read Maimonides?" in *Islam, Judaism and Christianity*, ed. John Inglis (Milton Park, UK: Taylor and Francis, 2002), 250–260.

38. B. Landry, *Duns Scotus* (Paris: Felix Alcan, 1922), 314–315.

39. M. Dykmans, Les sermons de Jean XXII sur la vision béatifique (Rome: Università Gregoriana editrice, 1973); Maimonides, *Guide of the Perplexed*, I:50.

40. Quoted in Yossef Schwartz, "Meister Eckhart and Moses Maimonides: From Judaeo-Arabic Rationalism to Christian Mysticism," in *A Companion to Meister Eckhart*, ed. Jeremiah M. Hackett (Leiden: Brill, 2013,) 414.

41. Maimonides, *Guide of the Perplexed*, II:30; I:2.

42. John Milton, "The Doctrine and Discipline of Divorce," chap. 6, in *The Works of John Milton*, ed. Frank Allen Patterson and Others (New York: Columbia University Press, 1931–1938), 3:402–440. The Maimonides citation is *Guide of the Perplexed*, III:49.

43. John Maynard Keynes, "Newton the Man," in Keynes, *Essays in Biography* (London: Macmillan, 1961), 316.

44. H. McLachlan, introduction to Isaac Newton, *Theological Manuscripts*, ed. McLachlan (Liverpool: Liverpool University Press, 1950), 13–17.

45. See Oded Cohen, "Eager to Belong—A Palestinian Jew in Eighteenth-Century Amsterdam," *Studia Rosenthaliana* 46, nos. 1–2, special issue: *The Jewish Bookshop of the World Aspects of Print and Manuscript Culture in Early Modern Amsterdam* (2020): 211–228.

46. Quoted in Daniel Cook, "Leibniz and 'Orientalism,'" *Studia Leibnitiana* 40, no. 2 (2008) 168–190.

47. Gottfried Wilhelm Leibniz, "Monadology," in *Philosophical Writings*, ed. and trans. G. H. R. Parkinson (London: Dent, 1973), 57. Leibniz is referencing Maimonides' *Guide*, I:72.

48. Gottfried Wilhelm Leibniz, *New Essays on Human Understanding* [1704], ed. and trans. Jonathan Francis Bennett and Peter Remnant (Cambridge: Cambridge University Press, 1996), 70.

49. Robert Burton, *The Anatomy of Melancholy*, ed. Holbrook Jackson (New York: New York Review Books, 2001), 245; John Donne, *Sermons* (Berkeley: University of California Press, 1962), 4:102.

50. George Berkeley, *The Principles of Human Knowledge. First Draft of the Introduction to the Principles. Three Dialogues Between Hylas and Philonous. Philosophical Correspondence with Johnson: Part 1*, in *The Works of George Berkeley, Bishop of Cloyne*, 9 vols., ed. A. A. Luce and T. E. Jessop (London: Thomas Nelson and Sons, 1948–1957) 2:211–212.

51. Georg Wilhelm Friedrich Hegel, "The Metaphysics of the Understanding, " sect. 2, in *Lectures on the History of Philosophy* [1896], trans. and ed. Robert F. Brown (Oxford: Oxford University Press, 2009), 3:283.

52. Marilena Chaui, "Notas preliminares para uma comparação entre Maimonides e Espinosa," *Cadernos Espoinosanos* 33 (2015): 15–41; Jorge Luis Borges, "Spinoza," in *El otro, el mismo* (Buenos Aires: Emecé, 1964), 78.

53. Maimonides, *Mishneh Torah*, Sefer Madda, Human Dispositions, 6.3.

54. Talmud, Shabbat 31a.

55. Baruch Spinoza, *Theological-Political Treatise*, trans. Samuel Shirley, 2nd ed. (Indianapolis: Hackett, 2001), 153.

56. Spinoza, *Theological-Political Treatise*, 27. Karl Jaspers suggested that Spinoza did not mean that God was to be identified with a static or passive nature, but rather with a dynamic nature in action, growing and changing.

57. Quoted in Michah Gottlieb, *Faith and Freedom: Moses Mendelssohn's Theological-political Thought* (New York: Oxford University Press, 2011), 88.

58. Quoted in Elias Sacks, "Civic Freedom out of the Sources of Judaism: Mendelssohn, Maimonides and Law's Promise," *Journal of Jewish Ethics* 2, no. 1 (2016): 88.

59. See Nadler, "The 'Rambam Revival' in Early Modern Jewish Thought," 45.

60. Quoted in James H. Lehmann, "Maimonides, Mendelssohn and the Me'asfim: Philosophy and Biographical Imagination in the Early Haskalah," *Leo Baeck Institute Year Book* 20, no. 1 (1987): 89.

61. Quoted in Nadler, "The 'Rambam Revival' in Early Modern Jewish Thought," 45; quoted in Lehmann, "Maimonides, Mendelssohn and the Me'asfim," 93.

62. Quoted in Lehmann, "Maimonides, Mendelssohn and the Me'asfim," 98–100.

63. See Nadler, "The 'Rambam Revival' in Early Modern Jewish Thought," 48.

64. Denis Diderot et Jean le Rond d'Alembert, *L'Encyclopédie* (Paris, 1765), 9:43; Diderot, *Pensées philosophique et Additions aux pensées philosophiques* (1746) (Paris: Flammarion, 2007), 161.

65. Voltaire, *Lettres à Son Altesse Monseigneur le Prince de *****. *Sur Rabelais & sur d'autres auteurs accusés d'avoir mal parlé de la religion chrétienne* (Amsterdam, chez Marc Michel Rey, 1767), Letter 9, p. 116; Voltaire, *Essay sur l'Histoire générale, et sur les mœurs et l'esprit des nations, depuis Charlemagne jusqu'a nos jours*, bk. 3, chap. 99 (Geneva: Cramer, 1761), 129.

66. See Nadler, "The 'Rambam' Revival in Early Modern Jewish Thought," 39.

67. Solomon Maimon, *The Autobiography of Solomon Maimon*, ed. Yitzhak Y. Melamed and Abraham Socher, trans. Paul Reitter (Princeton: Princeton University Press, 2018), 158–159.

68. George Y. Kohler, *Reading Maimonides' Philosophy in 19th Century Germany: The Guide to Religious Reform* (Dordrecht: Springer, 2012), 249.

69. Immanuel Kant, *Critique of Pure Reason*, trans. Norman Kemp Smith (London: Macmillan, 1982), 417–421.

70. See Leo Strauss, *Philosophy and Law: Essays Toward the Understanding of Maimonides and His Predecessors*, trans. Fred Baumann (Philadelphia: Jewish Publication Society, 1987), 81–110.

71. Jacob Fromer, *Maimonides Commentar zum Tractat Middoth: mit der hebräischen Uebersetzung des Natanel Almoli: kritische Ausgabe mit Anmerkungen und Zeichnungen* (Breslau: Theodor Schatzky, 1898), 41.

72. Franz Kafka, diary entry of 16 January 1922, in *Franz Kafka: The Diaries, 1910–1923*, ed. Max Brod (New York: Schocken, 1948), 399; Kafka, *Letters to Felice*, ed. Erich Heller and Jürgen Born, trans. James Stern and Elisabeth Duckworth (New York: Schocken, 1973), 690.

73. Maimonides, *Guide of the Perplexed*, III:24.

74. Richard Ellman, *James Joyce*, rev. ed. (Oxford: Oxford University Press, 1982), 501; James Joyce, *Ulysses* (1922; New York: Vintage, 1990), 683. Maimonides appears also in the chapter Oxen of the Sun cited together with Averroës as two authorities on the cir-

cumstances under which women can get pregnant without intercourse: for instance, in the bath. This was Joyce's invention: such a conjecture indeed appears in Averroës, but Maimonides the physician would not have endorsed such a superstitious conceit. Joyce might, however, have known that Maimonides laid out the rules of sexual interaction between husband and wife and argued that many kinds of relationship were permitted "as long as the act is consensual and does not occur in excess." Maimonides instructs that a person should not have intercourse while thinking of somebody else, or while drunk, in the midst of a fight, when that person is asleep, or hates the other, or after a man has decided in his heart to divorce his wife. Maimonides explicitly states that "the husband should not force his wife to have intercourse against her will or if she is afraid of him" (Maimonides, *Mishneh Torah*, Sefer Kedushah, Forbidden Intercourse, 21.9–12). Bloom might have been interested in the fact that, according to Maimonides, the husband can have vaginal or anal intercourse whenever he wishes (as long as his wife is permissible to him) and kiss any part of his wife's body he wishes. In the Lestrygonians chapter, Bloom recalls his lovemaking to his wife Molly, kissing her "eyes, her lips, her stretched neck beating, woman's breasts full in her blouse of nun's veiling, fat nipples upright" (Joyce, *Ulysses*, 314).

75. See *Borges, libros y lecturas: catálogo de la colección Jorge Luis Borges en la Biblioteca Nacional*, ed. Laura Rosato and Germán Álvarez, 2nd ed. (Buenos Aires: Ediciones Biblioteca Nacional, 2017).

76. Jorge Luis Borges, "Argumentum ornithologicum," in *El hacedor* (Buenos Aires: Emecé, 1960), 10.

77. Jorge Luis Borges, "El milagro secreto," in *Ficciones* (1944), in *Obras completas* (Buenos Aires: Sudamericana, 2011), 1:810.

78. Max Jammer, *Einstein and Religion: Physics and Theology* (Princeton: Princeton University Press, 2002), 143–149.

79. Quoted in Yosef Hayim Yerushalmi, *Zakhor: Jewish History and Jewish Memory* (Seattle: University of Washington Press, 1989), 111.

80. Maimonides, *The Eight Chapters of Maimonides on Ethics (Shemonah Peraḳim): A Psychological and Ethical Treatise*, trans. Jo-

seph I. Gorfinkle (New York: Columbia University Press, 1912), 38; David Bakan, Daniel Merkur, and David S. Weiss, *Maimonides' Cure of Souls: Medieval Precursor of Psychoanalysis* (Albany: State University of New York Press, 2009), 73.

81. Sigmund Freud, *Moses and Monotheism*, trans. Katherine Jones (London: Hogarth Press, 1939), 197.

82. C. G. Jung, *Mysterium Coniunctionis: An Inquiry into the Separation and Synthesis of Psychic Opposites in Alchemy*, trans. R. F. C. Hull, 2nd ed. (Princeton: Princeton University Press, 1963), 554.

83. Maimonides, *Guide of the Perplexed*, I:2, I:30, III:8 III:27, III:28, III:51, and III:54.

84. Jung, *Mysterium Coniunctionis*, 398.

85. C. G. Jung, *Aion: Researches into the Phenomenology of the Self*, trans. R. F. C. Hull, 2nd ed. (Princeton: Princeton University Press, 1959), 118–119.

86. Jacques Lacan, *Le séminaire, livre XVII: L'envers de la psychanalyse, 1969–1970*, ed. Jacques-Alain Miller, trans. Russell Grigg (New York: Norton, 2004), 158.

87. See Georges Leroux, "Passion transcendance: Derrida, lecteur du platonisme négatif," *Études françaises* 38 (2002): 87–102.

88. Cristian Ciocan and Georges Hansel, *Levinas Concordance* (Dordrechet: Springer, 2005), 903–916.

89. See Michael Fagenblat, "From Metaphysics to Ethical Negative Theory," *Journal of Jewish Thought and Philosophy* 16, no. 1 (2008): 95–147.

90. Maimonides, *Guide of the Perplexed*, I:59; Emmanuel Levinas, *Totalité et infini: Essai sur l'exteriorité* (Paris: Seuil, 1961), 43: "Aborder Autrui dans le discours, c'est accueillir son expression où il déborde à tout instant l'idée qu'en emporterait une pensée. C'est donc recevoir d'Autrui au-delà de la capacité du Moi; ce qui signifie exactement : avoir l'idée de l'infini. Mais cela signifie aussi être enseigné."

91. Ilana Maymind, *Exile and Otherness: The Ethics of Shinran and Maimonides* (Lanham, Md.: Lexington, 2020).

92. See Dong Xiuyuan, "Maimonides and Zhu Xi on the Role of Classical Norms in the Pursuit of Human Perfection," *Journal*

of Chinese Philosophy 45, nos. 3–4 (September–December 2018): 190–206.

93. Quoted in Carlo Ossola, *Nœuds: Figures de l'essentiel* (Paris: Éditions Collège de France, 2021), 18.

Conclusion

1. J. Diaz, "Anti-Semitic Incidents Surged in 2019, Report Says," *New York Times*, 12 May 2020.

2. Michael Kaminer, "Survey: One in Three Spaniards is Anti-Semitic," *Forward*, 14 September 2010, https://forward.com /schmooze/131234/survey-one-in-three-spaniards-is-anti-semitic/.

3. Maimonides, *The Guide of the Perplexed*, trans. Shlomo Pines, 2 vols. (Chicago: University of Chicago Press, 1963), III:51.

4. Talmud, Bava Metzia 59b.

PRINCIPAL WORKS BY MAIMONIDES

Works on Philosophy and Theology

Epistle on Conversion (or *Martyrdom*), or *Iggeret ha-Shemad*. (Some scholars doubt this attribution.)

Epistle to Yemen, or *Iggeret Teiman*, a letter to Rabbi Jacob al-Fayyumi on the critical condition of the Jews in Yemen (1172).

The Guide of the Perplexed, or *Dalalat al-Ḥa'irin*. Translated into Hebrew by Samuel ibn Tibbon in 1204 under the title *Moreh Nevukhim*.

Treatise on Logical Terminology, or *Maḳalah fi-Ṣina'at al-Manṭik*, on the terminology of logic, written at the age of sixteen (though this is disputed). It was translated into Hebrew under the title *Millot ha-Higgayon* and was first published, with two anonymous commentaries, in Venice in 1552.

Works on Halakhah

Commentary on the Mishnah, or *Kitab al-Siraj*.

Commentary on Hullin: Of this commentary, which Maimonides cites in the introduction to the Mishnah, only the section on "Rosh ha-Shanah" is known.

Mishneh Torah, or *Yad ha-Ḥazakah*.

Scientific Works

Commentary on Hippocrates' Aphorisms Extracted from the Commentary of Galen.

An Essay on the Jewish Calendar, Based on Astronomical Principles or *Ma'amar ha-Ibbur*.

Essays on Hygiene, or *Consultations with Malik al-Faḍl, son of Saladin*.

On Hemorrhoids, or *Fi al-Bawaṣir*.

On Sexual Intercourse, or *Fi al-Jama'ah*.

On the Case of the Prince of Rikka, or *Makalah fi Biyan al-A'raḍ*, translated into Hebrew anonymously under the title *Teshubot 'al She'elot Peraṭiyyot*.

On Various Poisons and Their Antidotes, or *Al-Sumum wal-Mutaharriz Min al-Adwiyyah al-Ḳitalah* (also known as *Al-Makalah al-Faḍiliyyah*).

Correspondence

Maimonides' *Correspondence* and some consultations appeared at first without place or date, and later under the title *Teshubot She'elot we-Iggarot* in Constantinople (1520). His responsa were translated from the Arabic into Hebrew by Mordecai Tammah and published in Amsterdam (1765) under the title *Pe'er ha-Dor*, and in Leipzig (1859) under the title *Ḳobeẓ Teshubot Rambam*.

ACKNOWLEDGMENTS

HEARTFELT THANKS TO Ileene Smith, editorial director of the Jewish Lives series, and John Donatich, director of Yale University Press, for entrusting me with this biography, five long years ago, and for their confident patience. And to Heather Gold for her support. Also to the proofreader Erica Hanson, the indexer Enid Zafran, and the picture researcher Suzie Tibor.

Thanks to my agents, Guillermo Schavelzon and Bárbara Graham, and their always supportive team.

Thanks to the Writers' Trust of Canada for their invaluable help in finishing this book.

Thanks to Karen Mulhallen for her love and friendship, *semper fidelis.*

Thanks, as usual, to Susan Laity, for her impeccable editorial reading. Had she been present in Maimonides' time, none of the Rambam's critics could have leveled against him the charges of obscurity, lack of exact bibliographical sources, and perhaps even the occasional typo in his manuscripts.

Thanks to Jillian Tomm, dearest of friends and meticulous reader, for her encouragement, comments and corrections. And simply for being there, always.

My deepest, most sincere thanks to my friend Arthur Kiron, who helped me comply with the instructions laid out in Mishnah, Tractate Avot 1:6. Without his keen, kind, erudite eye this book would never dared come into being.

As always, thanks to Craig, my *zivug*, without whom life past and present would not be conceivable.

INDEX

Illustrations are indicated by page numbers in italics.

JEWISH LIVES is a prizewinning series of interpretative biography designed to explore the many facets of Jewish identity. Individual volumes illuminate the imprint of Jewish figures upon literature, religion, philosophy, politics, cultural and economic life, and the arts and sciences. Subjects are paired with authors to elicit lively, deeply informed books that explore the range and depth of the Jewish experience from antiquity to the present.

Jewish Lives is a partnership of Yale University Press and the Leon D. Black Foundation. Ileene Smith is editorial director. Anita Shapira and Steven J. Zipperstein are series editors.

Lillian Hellman: An Imperious Life, by Dorothy Gallagher

Theodor Herzl: The Charismatic Leader, by Derek Penslar

Abraham Joshua Heschel: A Life of Radical Amazement,
    by Julian Zelizer

Houdini: The Elusive American, by Adam Begley

Jabotinsky: A Life, by Hillel Halkin

Jacob: Unexpected Patriarch, by Yair Zakovitch

Franz Kafka: The Poet of Shame and Guilt, by Saul Friedländer

Rav Kook: Mystic in a Time of Revolution, by Yehudah Mirsky

Stanley Kubrick: American Filmmaker, by David Mikics

Stan Lee: A Life in Comics, by Liel Leibovitz

Primo Levi: The Matter of a Life, by Berel Lang

Maimonides: Faith in Reason, by Alberto Manguel

Groucho Marx: The Comedy of Existence, by Lee Siegel

Karl Marx: Philosophy and Revolution, by Shlomo Avineri

Menasseh ben Israel: Rabbi of Amsterdam, by Steven Nadler

Moses Mendelssohn: Sage of Modernity, by Shmuel Feiner

Harvey Milk: His Lives and Death, by Lillian Faderman

Arthur Miller: American Witness, by John Lahr

Moses: A Human Life, by Avivah Gottlieb Zornberg

Proust: The Search, by Benjamin Taylor

Yitzhak Rabin: Soldier, Leader, Statesman, by Itamar Rabinovich

Walther Rathenau: Weimar's Fallen Statesman, by Shulamit Volkov

Man Ray: The Artist and His Shadows, by Arthur Lubow

Sidney Reilly: Master Spy, by Benny Morris

Admiral Hyman Rickover: Engineer of Power, by Marc Wortman

Jerome Robbins: A Life in Dance, by Wendy Lesser

Julius Rosenwald: Repairing the World, by Hasia R. Diner

Mark Rothko: Toward the Light in the Chapel, by Annie Cohen-Solal

Ruth: A Migrant's Tale, by Ilana Pardes

Gershom Scholem: Master of the Kabbalah, by David Biale

Bugsy Siegel: The Dark Side of the American Dream,
    by Michael Shnayerson
Solomon: The Lure of Wisdom, by Steven Weitzman
Steven Spielberg: A Life in Films, by Molly Haskell
Alfred Stieglitz: Taking Pictures, Making Painters, by Phyllis Rose
Barbra Streisand: Redefining Beauty, Femininity, and Power,
    by Neal Gabler
Leon Trotsky: A Revolutionary's Life, by Joshua Rubenstein
Warner Bros: The Making of an American Movie Studio,
    by David Thomson
Elie Wiesel: Confronting the Silence, by Joseph Berger

FORTHCOMING TITLES INCLUDE:

Abraham, by Anthony Julius
Hannah Arendt, by Masha Gessen
Walter Benjamin, by Peter Gordon
Franz Boas, by Noga Arikha
Alfred Dreyfus, by Maurice Samuels
Anne Frank, by Ruth Franklin
Betty Friedan, by Rachel Shteir
George Gershwin, by Gary Giddins
Allen Ginsberg, by Ed Hirsch
Herod, by Martin Goodman
Jesus, by Jack Miles
Josephus, by Daniel Boyarin
Louis Kahn, by Gini Alhadeff
Mordecai Kaplan, by Jenna Weissman Joselit
Carole King, by Jane Eisner
Fiorello La Guardia, by Brenda Wineapple
Hedy Lamarr, by Sarah Wildman
Mahler, by Leon Botstein